UNDERSTANDING RELIGION AND CULTURE:

Anthropological and Theological Perspecitves

Edited by
John H. Morgan
University of Texas

University Press
of America™

UNDERSTANDING RELIGION AND CULTURE:

Anthropological and Theological Perspectives

Edited by   John H. Morgan
University of Texas

Essays by   John P. Thorp
St. Mary's College

James Preston
State University of New York-Oneonta

E. Jean Langdon
Cedar Crest College

Ann Marie Powers
SUNY-Stony Brook

Fritz Holscher
University of South Africa

James O. Buswell, III
Wheaton College

Alice Higman Reich
Regis College

John H. Morgan

DEDICATION

To Professor Clifford Geertz,

in genuine admiration and

critical appreciation

ACKNOWLEDGEMENTS

Countless people, places, and circumstances have contributed to this project, and though this editor will not attempt to identify all of them, some must be. First and most importantly, I must express sincere appreciation to Professor Bhabagrahi Misra, my anthropology teacher during those delightful days of graduate study who called my attention to the writings of Clifford Geertz. To Professor Dennison Nash of the Anthropology Department of the University of Connecticut who let me teach my first graduate course in anthropology, I am deeply appreciative. My two appointments at Yale University provided the first real opportunity to consider the possibility of collecting essays from young scholars to honor as best we could the work of Geertz. My year as Scholar-in-Residence at The University of Chicago made possible the writing of an exploratory essay comparing Geertz and Paul Tillich, but only recently did Professor Geertz inform me from Oxford that he had regularly attended the lectures of Tillich during the time they were both at Harvard. Finally, my postdoctoral appointment as Visiting Fellow at Princeton provided a genuine opportunity to bring the following project to fruition. To my fellow contributors, I am appreciative for their patience and understanding during the hectic days of collecting and editing. Without the encouragement and support, even when I was far from pleasant, of my wife, Linda, and our three daughters, Kendra, Bethany, and Kyna, this project nor any of my other ventures worthwhile would have ever reached completion.

PREFACE

The essays collected in this volume have been written in honor of Clifford Geertz, Professor of Social Science at Princeton's Institute for Advanced Studies. Professor Geertz, who is spending a year abroad as Distinguished Eastman Professor at Oxford University, is America's foremost anthropologist of Religion and today is the most quoted scholar in his field. Geertz, a product of Harvard University where he had occasion to attend the lectures of the late professor of theology and culture, Paul Tillich, has spent much of his academic life struggling with the analysis of the complex relationship between religion and culture, and though his methodological and theoretical agenda has been that of an anthropologist, the philosophical and theological implications of his work have been profound. The essays collected here range from ethnographic analysis employing Geertz's methodology to theological evaluations of the importance of Geertz's theory of religion. The essays have been written by primarily young scholars in anthropology and theologians who have been influenced by Geertz's scholarship. Though all indicate the importance of his theories for their understanding of religion and culture, some are most supportive while others are somewhat critical. All concur that Geertz has not only greatly assisted them in their understanding of these complex phenomena but that he is without doubt the most important theoritician in this field of study on the contemporary scene. The facilitation of dialogue between anthropologists and theologians and the better understanding of the issues involved in the study of religion and culture constitute the primary impetus of these essays in honor of Clifford Geertz.

TABLE OF CONTENTS

CHAPTER ONE

"Clifford Geertz: An Interfacing of Anthropology

and Religious Studies,"

John H. Morgan
University of Texas

ABSTRACT

Clifford Geertz is acclaimed today to be one of the most important theorists in the anthropology of religion. He has approached the subject-matter of religion from that of a humanist seeking to come to an analytical understanding of the nature of culture as an historically transmitted pattern of meanings embodied in a complex of symbol-systems. This approach, i.e., defining anthropology as a science of meaning-analysis, nurtures the study of culture as a meaning-system. Religion, too, says Geertz, is a cultural system and necessarily conveys meaning. Therefore, both culture and religion are meaning-systems and, we can conclude, both anthropology and theology attempt to analyze systematically these meaning-systems. The interfacing of the disciplines of anthropology (systematics of culture) and theology (systematics of religion) is made possible by the utilization of the category of "meaning" as a hermeneutical key to the understanding of both religion and culture as meaning-systems.

*In an attempt to blaze a humanistic path between positivism and functionalism, Geertz has put forth what is increasingly being considered the most useful definition of religion to-date in the social sciences. "The view of man as a symbolizing, conceptualizing, meaning-seeking animal opens a whole new approach to the analysis of religion," says Geertz.[1] While attempting to demonstrate the legitimate perimeters of the social sciences, and especially anthropology, in analyzing religious phenomena, Geertz conscientiously with-holds any challenge to the methodological credibility of the history and phenomenology of religions in their pursuit of the essence of religious experience. He has put forth the following definition: "Religion is (1) a system of symbols which acts to (2) establish powerful, persuasive, and long-lasting moods and motiviations in men by (3) formulating conceptions of a general order of existence and (4) clothing these conceptions with such an aura of factuality that (5) the moods and motivations seem uniquely realistic."[2] The design, obviously, is not to construct a definitive definition which exhausts all dimensions of religious phenomena (how absurd such a notion would be!), but rather to construct a realistic and useable definition with intentional limitations and specificity of scope.

Concurring with but not limiting himself to Yinger's definition of religion as a "system of beliefs and practices by means of which a group of people struggles with ultimate problems of human life,"[3] Geertz suggests that a fundamental characteristic of religion is the address to the "problem of meaning" — meaning suggesting pur-

*This essay is a a revision of a paper I presented before the 1977 American Anthropological Association's Annual Meeting in Houston. Special thanks are expressed to The University of Chicago and Princeton where I held successive postdoctoral research appointments during which time this research was undertaken.

purpose and direction to life and meaninglessness suggesting chaos and pointless existence. "There are at least three points," says Geertz, "where chaos — a tumult of events which lack not just interpretation but interpretability — threatens to break in upon man at the limits of his analytic capacities, at the limits of his powers of endurance, and at the limits of his moral insight. Bafflement, suffering, and a sense of intractable ethical paradox are all radical challenges with which any religion, however 'primitive,' which hopes to persist must attempt somehow to cope."[4] Without doing violence to the social scientific perspective of Geertz, we can say that religion constitutes an experientially motivated address to the problem of impending chaos in the existential experience of humankind. Furthermore, we can say that beyond, behind, or under religion's capacity to cope with bafflement, suffering, and inextricable ethical paradox lies the "essence of meaning" to which these expressions in quest of existential meaning are enduring witnesses. This implied extension cannot, of course, be pursued in this study, but I have considered it at length in another place.[5]

Geertz is not oblivious to this possible extension and logical elaboration of his position, nor is he antipathetic to such an endeavor. "The Problem of Meaning in each of its intergrading aspects," continues Geertz, "is a matter of affirming, or at least recognizing, the inescapability of ignorance, pain, and injustice on the human plane while simultaneously denying that these irrationalities are characteristic of the world as a whole."[6] Even an elementary acquaintance with the history of the

— 3 —

scientific study of religion is sufficient to establish the qualitative advance Geertz's definition has made, especially as he employs the concept of meaning as an interpretive key. Within his definitional construct Geertz stands head and shoulders above recent efforts to understand religion by the positivists and functionalists. With his efforts, the way is truly open for an honest dialogue between the social scientists and theologians. "The existence," Geertz concludes, "of bafflement, pain and moral paradox — of the Problem of Meaning — is one of the things that drive men toward belief in gods, devils, spirits, totemic principles, or the spiritual efficacy of cannibalism, but it is not the basis upon which those beliefs rest, but rather their most important field of application."[7] This "drive toward belief" is conveyed through cultural symbols and bespeaks man's quest for meaning, for an existential meaning which challenges chaos and which pursues order. "Whatever else religion may be," Geertz says, "it is in part an attempt (of an implicit and directly felt rather than explicit and consciously thought-about sort) to conserve the fund of general meanings in terms of which each individual interprets his experience and organizes his conduct . . ."[8]

MEANING AS HERMENEUTICS

Culture and religion are both symbol-systems which express humankind's quest for meaning. Therefore, any serious convergence of cultural and religious expressions necessarily centers around the experience of meaning, an experience which is multidimensional and expressed through symbols.[9] Though culture is historically trans-

mitted as _patterns of meaning_ which are embodied in a "complex of symbols,"
Geertz contends that "meanings can only be 'stored' in symbols," and are not sy-
nonymous with the symbols themselves. Positivists attempt to equate "meanings"
with symbols themselves, while functionalists attempt to equate the social "functions" of meaning-symbols with meanings themselves. Whereas culture and religion
are convergent _expressions of meaning_, anthropology and theology are disciplines
addressed to the _systematics of meaning_, and as noted above, the analysis of meaning will inevitably involve an analysis of the symbol as meaning-bearer.[10]

Religion as studied by anthropologists involves a two-step operation, according
to Geertz: "First, an analysis of the system of meanings embodied in the symbols
which make up the religion proper, and second, the relating of these systems to
social-structural and psychological processes."[11] Geertz has consistently demonstrated a receptiveness to the various disciplinary approaches to religious studies,
including phenomenology as the study of "religion proper," and has suggested a
model for multi-disciplinary complementarity. _Anthropology is an interpretive
science_ engaged in the _search for meaning_ through a _systematic analysis of culture_,
i.e., the study of human meanings embodied in symbols. "The concept of culture
I espouse," explains Geertz, "and whose utility the essays below (in his collected
works) attempt to demonstrate, is essentially a semiotic one."[12] "Analysis," continues Geertz, "is sorting out the structures of significance and determining their
ground and import."[13]

In another place, Geertz has said, "The culture concept to which I adhere denotes an historically transmitted pattern of meanings embodied in symbols, a system of inherited conceptions expressed in symbolic forms by means of which men communicate, perpetuate, and develop their knowledge about and attitudes toward life."[14] If culture, then, is the expression of meaning, and anthropology is the analysis of culture, we can say that the fundamental task of anthropology put succinctly is the systematics of meaning. And this systematic analysis, or systematization of meaning, necessitates an analysis of the socio-cultural structures and processes which constitute the framework of meaning. This systems analysis approach implies interpretation, or more correctly, hermeneutics.[15] If culture is the experience and expression of meaning (or rather the context within which and the socio-historical mechanism whereby meaning is both experienced and expressed), then the function of the concept of meaning necessarily is interpretational, or hermeneutical, and in turn, anthropology constitutes the analytical mechanism for identifying and systematizing meaning such as to serve as an effective interpretation of human culture. In other words, culture is meaning and meaning is hermeneutics.

An essential quality of the anthropological enterprise is its desire for universal application. The cross-cultural perspective is the sine qua non of anthropological method. The desired benefit in the employment of anthropological method is the facilitation of what Geertz has called "the enlargment of the universe of human discourse." Anthropology's sensitivity to the vast panorama of human experience exemplified in a substantially built up collection of cross-cultural studies plays a vital role in establishing the discipline's capacity to interpret meaning-systems. In any anthropological analysis of culture patterns, there is an attempt to observe and understand "the degree to which its meaning (i.e., culture's) varies according to the pattern of life by which it is informed."[16] We are confronted with three alternative responses to this anthropological approach to the analysis of culture and religion: (1) To be impressed with the dynamics of cultural diversity while vigorously pursuing the analysis of various culture forms and contents yet foregoing any philosophical speculation as to the implications of such an impression, (2) to be so impressed with cultural diversity that one concludes that life has no "ground" and the only absolute is "relativity," or (3) to be informed by cultural diversity as form-and-content expressions of meaning which are understood to be reflections of meaning-reality. The discipline of anthropology, when strictly adhering to its definition as a science for the systematic analysis of socio-cultural phenomena, is bound to the first option – observation, description, understanding, and interpretation. Nowhere is the discipline forced to adhere either to the second or third options and when it does, it either steps into the circle of positivism (in the second option) or philosophy (in the third option).

We can discount the second option from this discussion as antipathetic to the integrity of anthropology as a social science. (The second option, where tenaciously held to, would result in anthropology's demotion to a mere ideological sect.) From the very outset of our inquiry, we have understood Geertz to be suggesting that anthropology, defined in terms of the first option, when engaged in a dialogue with theology could fruitfully lead to an interfacing of methods suggested in the third option – a method of religio-cultural analysis. Geertz is clear in his portrayal of the vocation of anthropology appropriate to this point:

> To look at the symbolic dimensions of social action – art, religion, ideology, science, law, morality, common sense – is not to turn away from the existential dilemmas of life for some empyrean realm of de-emotionalized forms; it is to plunge into the midst of them. The essential vocation of interpretive anthropology is not to answer our deepest questions, but to make available to us answers that others, guarding other sheep in other valleys, have given, and thus to include them in the consultable record of what man has said.[17]

We need not attempt a resolution here of the age-old philosophical dispute over whether the presence of order is in the world and thus discoverable or whether order is in the mind and thus constructable. The answer to such a problem, though certainly desirable, is not a prerequisite to our observation about man being driven to find/create order-system-category. This drive is suggestive of an imperative in human experience – no society exists without a conception of order in the world or of system in experience. Within religious community, suggests Geertz, sacred symbols function to synthesize that community's "worldview" (structure of reality – metaphysics) and its "ethos" (style of life – values).[18] "The drive to make sense out of experience, to give it form and order," says Geertz, "is evidently as real and as pressing as the more familiar biological needs." This making "sense out of experience" is what we are calling here the systematics of meaning. Though Geertz and another noteworthy social scientist, Peter L. Berger, seem to have resolved for themselves the issue of finding-or-creating order, we need not pass judgement upon that personal preference to concur with this apparent human imperative to order and systematize. "Men are congenitally compelled," suggests Berger, "to impose a meaningful order upon reality."[19] "One fundamental human trait which is of crucial importance in understanding man's religious enterprise," says Berger in another place, "is his propensity for order."[20]

As we have seen, religion and culture are intergrative expressions of meaning. Nevertheless, there is admittedly more to meaning than just its experientially-based expressions. Mankind has always sought to organize his expressions of meaning and no society has ever been devoid of systematizers, as Radin pointed out years ago. "There can be little doubt," Radin observed, "that every group, no matter how small, has, from time immemorial, contained individuals who were constrained by their individual termpaments to occupy themselves with the basic problems of what we customarily term philosophy."[21] And, as with philosophy, so with anthropology, i.e., man's unabated effort to understand and interpret the meaning of life. "Hence," says Geertz in another effort to illustrate the interpretive nature of the science of anthropology, "any scientific approach to the study of symbols (anthropology is essentially a refined science of symbolism) is interpretive in nature. It is a search for meaning which results in an explication of the symbol. In short, anthropological writings are themselves interpretations, and second and third order ones to boot."[22]

In our investigation of the possibilities of interfacing anthropology and theology, Geertz's definition of anthropology as an "interpretive science" has given rise to a characterization of anthropology as the systematic analysis of culture-as-meaning. It can also be suggested that, in an attempt to understand religion-as-meaning, the human propensity for order gives rise to an intellectual interest in the systematic analysis of religion-as-meaning. The social scientific approach to the study of religion, as demonstrated in Geertz, is a systematic analysis of the content and forms of religious and cultural phenomena. Geertz says anthropology does not seek to understand the "basis of belief" but rather belief's manifestations. The task of analyzing and systematizing the "basis of belief" resides squarely in the lap of theologians and philosophers.

Human experience finds expression through the meaning-systems of culture and religion. The analysis of experientially stimulated meaning-expressions and the systematization of this analytic enterprise has occupied our time throughout this deliberation. That we have defined religion and culture in terms of the category of experience must, says Geertz, necessarily inform our definition of anthropology. More precisely, Geertz nurtures an anthropological method which is concentrated upon experiential meaning as the key to understanding both culture and religion. From this we can argue that both religion and culture are meaning and meaning is hermeneutics.

Admittedly, Geertz is not a theologian. He is not even engaging consciously or otherwise in the theological task. As an anthropologist, he is attempting to come to a better understand of human behavior — its form, its content, its meaning. In this endeavor, he asserts that the experiential dynamic operative within and reflective through cultural expressions is fundamentally a dynamic of human "meaning." Culture, says Geertz, is a complex interplay of symbols expressing meaning. Therefore, religion as a cultural system is also expressive of meaning, and an expression of Man's search for meaning. This meaning, found in and expressed by religious symbols and cultural systems, is demonstrative of mankind's quest to know and understand his world and his place in it. For theologians interested in the theological interfacing of religion and culture, for social scientists interested in the philosophical importance of "meaning" in socio-cultural analysis, and for religio-phenomenologists interested in the interdisciplinary possibilities between anthropology and philosophy, Geertz's work provides a singularly provocative example of such efforts done well.

FOOTNOTES

1. Clifford Geertz, "Ethos, World-View and the Analysis of Sacred Symbols," Antioch Review (Winter, 1957-58), 436. Other major works of Geertz include The religion of Java (Glencoe: The Free Press, 1960); Islam Observed (New Haven: Yale University Press, 1968); The Interpretation of Cultures (New York: Basic Books, 1973); Myth, Symbol, and Culture (New York: W. W. Norton, 1974), edited by Geertz; "Ideology as a Cultural System," in D. Apter (ed.), Ideology and Discontent (New York: The Free Press, 1964); "The Impact of the Concept of Culture on the Concept of Man," in J. Platt (ed.), New Views of the Nature of Man (Chicago: University Press, 1966); "The Growth of Culture and the Evolution of Mind," in J. Scher (ed.), Theories of the Mind (New York: The Pree Press, 1967); "Religion as a Cultural System," in M. Banton (ed.), Anthropological Approaches to the Study of Religion (London: Tavistock, 1966); and "The Politics of Meaning," in C. Holt (ed.), Culture and Politics in Indonesia (Ithica: Cornell University Press, 1972).

2. Geertz, "Religion as a Cultural System," p. 5.

3. J. Milton Yinger, The Scientific Study of Religion (N.Y.: Macmillan, 1970), p. 7.

4. Geertz, "Religion as a Cultural System," p. 14.

5. See my "Religion and Culture as Meaning Systems: A Dialogue Between Geertz and Tillich," The Journal of Religion, LVII, 4 (Oct., 1977), 363-375.

6. Geertz, "Religion as a Cultural System," p. 24.

7. Ibid., p. 25.

8. Geertz, "Ethos, World-View and the Analysis of Sacred Symbols," p. 422.

9, Ibid.

10. For a consideration of Ernst Cassirer's reference to man as an animal symbolicum, see my article, "Theology and Symbol: An Anthropological Approach," Journal of Religious Thought, XXX, 2 (Fall, 1974), 51-61; and also my article, "Religious Myth and Symbol: A Convergence of Philosphy and Anthropology," Philosophy Today, XVIII, 4 (Spring, 1974), 68-84.

11. Geertz, "Religion as a Cultural System," p. 42.

12. Geertz, The Interpretation of Cultures, p. 5.

13. Ibid., p. 9.

14. Geertz, "Religion as a Cultural System," p. 3.

15. A splendid assessment of the current state of philosophical hermeneutics is presented by Richard E. Palmer, Hermeneutics: Interpretation Theory (Evanston, Ill.: Northwestern University Press, 1969), especially his chapter on Heidegger.

16. Geertz, The Interpretation of Cultures, p. 14.

17. Ibid., p. 30.

18. Geertz, "Religion as a Cultural System," p. 23.

19. Peter L. Berger, The Sacred Canopy: Elements of a Sociological Theory of Religion (New York: Anchor, 1969), p. 22.

20. Peter L. Berger, A Rumor of Angels: Modern Society and the Rediscovery of the Sacred (New York: Anchor, 1970), p. 53.

21. Paul Radin, <u>Primitive Man as Philosophy</u> (New York: Dover, 1957), p xxi.

22. Geertz, <u>The Interpretation of Cultures</u>, pp. 5, 15.

CHAPTER TWO

"Bengali Muslims and the Symbolism of Earth: A

Geertzian Analysis"

John P. Thorp
St. Mary's College

ABSTRACT

The symbol system of the Muslims of rural Bangladesh is concretized in the story of Adam's creation from the earth. The earth (mati) is the core symbol in this system, and it serves as the vehicle for conceptualizing meaning, especially the meaning of power in this society. Earth and its complex of meanings is both a model of and a model for reality among these farmers.

INTRODUCTION

The farmers of Daripalla[1] are Bengali Muslims. Their perceptions of the world and their place in it are directly influenced by Islam. Islam has provided these farmers with a system of religious symbols by means of which they conceptualize a general order of existence which has an aura of absolute factuality for them, and which provides them with the sense that they are living in the "really real" world. The religious perceptions of these farmers provide them with the pervasive moods and motivations that characterize their way of life. Religion for the farmers of Daripalla is a cultural system, as Clifford Geertz has described it.[2]

The fundamental set of religious symbols which these farmers rely upon is drawn from the scattered Quranic references to Allah's creation of heaven and earth, angels and men.[3] However, these Bengli farmers tell a well-organized and highly developed creation story which expands upon the passing references to creation in the Quran. The story these farmers tell encapsulates a system of symbols which provides them with explanations of themselves and their world. In this paper I will, first, present a paraphrase of the creation story as told in Daripalla.[4] Then, I will elaborate upon the system of symbols contained in this story. Central to Daripallans' account of creation and to their explanations of themselves as human beings is the multivocal symbol of earth. By focusing my treatment upon this symbol I hope to introduce the reader to the system of religious symbols which provides these farmers with their sense of who they are, and what they are about.

THE DARIPALLAN STORY OF CREATION

According to the farmers of Daripalla, when Allah decided to create the world, he first took some of his own light (nur) and created the Prophet Muhammad[5]. From the light which he had infused in Muhammad Allah then created the four substances of earth, air, fire, and water. From different combinations of these substances Allah created heaven and the earth, and everything in these two realms. He peopled heaven with the angels which he created from fire. Taking some earth (mati) and mixing it with water Allah shaped the first human form. He infused this human form with some of the Prophet Muhammad's light, and then he gave it life (ruhu). Thus, was Adam created. For the moment Adam resided in heaven, but he was a radically different creature than the angels. Most importantly, Adam was talented (khamatasali), and the angels were not. As the farmers tell it, Adam was able to "learn the names" of everything in heaven and on earth much to the dismay of Iblis, the leader of the Angels. Iblis reasoned that since he was created before Adam and was created from fire, he was superior to Adam. He was the one who should have the ability to learn the names and purposes of all of Allah's creatures. As Allah showed more and more interest in Adam, creating a wife for him from a bone of his left side, Iblis became very jealous of Adam and his wife, Howa. Before too much longer, Allah informed Iblis that he was making Adam, his creature of earth, the master (malik) of the earth and all its contents. Iblis objected, but Allah silenced him, telling him that Adam was fit for this task because of his composition from the earth itself which rendered him skilled, talented and dynamic (khamatasali) beyond anything Iblis could hope to be. As the farmers of Daripalla stress, earth is superior to, and more powerful than fire. Furthermore, Allah informed Iblis that he and all the angels would have to show Adam honor and respect by bowing down before him. The other angels accepted this command, but Iblis flatly refused to obey Allah's command. He would not accept being Adam's inferior. Allah warned him that he would be put out of heaven to inhabit hell, if he did not submit and obey this command. Still, Iblis refused to bow down to Adam, and he was put out of heaven. Iblis took up his residence in hell, vowing all the while to make Adam disobey Allah's commands, and like himself suffer Allah's displeasure in hell. The farmers of Daripalla go on to tell how Iblis was successful in making Adam and Howa disobey Allah's command not to eat a certain plant in heaven, presumably wheat.. As a result of their eating this wheat, Adam and Howa began to urinate and defecate. Thus, their disobedience was immediately manifest in heaven. For this failure to obey Allah, Adam and Howa were put out of heaven and placed on earth. Adam was commanded to exercise his mastery over the earth in a skillful way so as to sustain himself, his wife and his offspring from the fruit of the earth. Allah also warned Adam not to disobey him in the future; he encouraged Adam to remain faithful to his commands, despite Iblis. Allah promised that Adam and his descendants would be kept informed of his commands. Ultimately, the Prophet Muhammad would reveal Allah's Law (sunna) to Adam's descendants.[6]. According to Allah's insructions Adam began to farm the earth and to bring forth from the earth food which sustained his physical strength (sakti) and his talents and ability (khamata). Howa too was nourished and sustained by this food. Together Adam and Howa produced many children who were born as sets of twins, a boy and a girl together. Adam's two oldest sons, Habel and Kabel, grew into men. Kabel was jealous of his older brother, Habel, who was an industrious farmer and obedient son. When Adam decided Habel should marry Kabel's twin sister, Kabel murdered his brother because of his jealousy. His sister was very beautiful, and he wanted her for himself. Once again Iblis had been successful in making a man disobedient. The Muslims of Daripalla claim Adam's good son, Habel, as their forebearer, and they attribute descent from Kabel to the Hindus. All the other peoples (jati) of the world (Christians, Buddhists, and Jews) have descended from other sons of Adam and Howa.

THE EARTH AS OBJECT AND SYMBOL

This creation story is a summary statement of Daripallans' symbol system. Although this story makes this system only partially explicit, nevertheless the story is significant because it serves as the focus of attention or the point of departure for Daripallans when they attempt to explain the world they live in. Religious teachers use it in their preaching. Adult males and females refer to it in discussions among themselves and in the instruction of their children. Children refer to it in their own intereactions. This anthropologist's informants regularly and spontaneously relied upon this story to enculturate him, and to answer his more pressing questions about the what, why, who, and how of their existence. Although Daripallans do not refer to it as a system of symbols, this story does contain the basic symbolic forms by means of which they communicate, perpetuate, and develop their knowledge about and attitudes toward life.[7] By viewing the various items from this story as symbolic forms the fullest sense can be made of Daripallans' own statements about themselves and their world.

Any object, act, event, quality, or relation which serves as a vehicle for a conception can be considered a symbol.[8] The objects, acts, events, relations and qualities referred to in the creation story serve as the vehicles for a number of conceptions. In fact, the story is a web or network of such symbolic interrelations. For Daripallans the central symbol in this network is that of the earth or soil (mati). In order to appreciate the earth as a symbol, the place of earth as a sensually perceptible object among Daripallans must first be appreciated. Earth is the single most important object in the lives of these people. They are farmers who obtain their subsistence by cultivating the earth. Obtaining food from the earth occupies most of their waking attention. Since Daripalla is a completely rural area of Bangladesh with the nearest town over eight miles away, this is not surprising. Although road communications with this town are good, no Daripallan is employed there. This, on the other hand, is noteworthy because forty per cent of the farmers in Daripalla do not possess any cultivable land of their own, although almost everyone does own his own household site. If Daripallans do not cultivate their own land, they labor upon the land of others. Even those few Daripallans who are completely destitute are dependent upon the productivity of the earth for those farmers from whom they beg.

As an object of the sensually perceptible world, earth is subject to careful and accurate classification by these farmers. Four major types of soil are distinguished: sandy, clayey, loamy, and gravelly soil. Particular fields are classified according to whether they contain one or other of these types of earth, or contain soil representing a combination of types. The different types of land have different properties and require different kinds of care in their cultivation. For example, much more fertilizer is necessary in the use of sandy soil. The gologic disposition of particular fields is also important in evaluating their potential productivity. Access to water and a field's susceptibility to flooding are a major concern. Five categories of land are distinguished basically on the criterion of height: high land, crop land, rice land, low land, and permanently inundated land. Individual farmers are accutely aware of the relationship between the soil type and the geologic disposition of each of their fields, and the productivity of each field given varying monsoon and dry season conditions. A skillful farmer in Daripalla can obtain as many as two rice crops and a dry season crop from some fields. If he schedules the use of his fields over a two-year cycle, he might even obtain one more crop. During the course of a year a farmer makes many decisions about which crops he will sow in which of his fields, such as rice or jute, vegetables or oil seeds. Like farmers everywhere he is concerned with maximizing his output and minimizing his risks of failure. The nature and disposition of the earth which a farmer possesses or controls is considered the most important variable in the equation which that person must manipulate in order to successfully produce food.

Not only does the earth or the soil produce food for Daripallans, but it also provides them with an important construction material. All the structures of rural Bengal make use of earth in some fashion. The ordinary structure is constructed with a raised earth floor hardened by the application of cow dung. Posts and wattle screens are constructed from bamboo. A mixture of earth and cow dung is used to plaster the interior and exterior walls. A special, though plentiful, tall grass is used for roofing. During the monsoon season from June through October frequent repairs must be made to the exterior mud plastering on most structures. A few structures of brick and concrete have been erected in the local bazaars and at the local government headquarters, but even here the earth provided the basic raw material for the bricks. The life style of Daripallans does not call for a great deal of furniture. With the exception of wooden plank beds, Daripallans are content without furniture. The earth provides their working surfaces and their resting places. Life in Daripalla is lived in intimate contact with and dependence upon the soil.

Unlike Western society which views such close contact with the earth as "dirty," Muslim Daripallans view their dependence upon and contact with the earth as positive and good. Although the Bengali lexicon as used in Daripalla contains separate lexemes for the substances 'earth' (mati), and the geographic entity the 'world' (duniya), nevertheless these Bengali farmers would appreciate the English usage wherein 'earth' stands for both the substance and the geographic entity composed of this substance. The world in which Daripallans live is truly and significantly one of earth. However, besides being a sensually perceptible and physically all-pervasive object of their experience, earth is also a vehicle for a number of conceptions which are central to Daripallans' cultural system. Earth is a symbol. The most significant association with earth in this context are conceptions of power. In Daripalla to talk of the earth is not simply to talk of an inert physical substance, but to talk of an empowered and empowering substance. Earth is considered the first of the four basic substances which Allah created from the Prophet Muhammad's light, which was itself a transformation of Allah's own light. Various combinations of these four substances by Allah produced the heavens and the earth. He used fire to create Iblis and the angels. Most significantly, however, he used the first substance, earth, to create Adam. Transformed through this substance was into flesh, bone, blood, semen, and Adam's other bodily fluids and substances, it was still the earth that constituted Adam as Allah's special creature. Earth determined both what Adam was and what he was not, and by implication what Daripallans are and are not.

First of all, it is necessary to consider briefly what Adam was not. To be created from earth separated Adam clearly and absolutely from Allah. Allah pre-existed and by the use of his own special and particular power (kudrat) brought Adam and all creatures into existence. Allah's own activity on a variety of sub-stances produced all that is, and Allah alone is capable of this creative activity. Possessed of kudrat Allah is Creator. Everything else is creature, the result of Allah's power and dependent upon it. Given the South Asian Hindu milieu in which this statement is made, the distinction is significant. Hindus in Bengal and throughout South Asia do not distinguish creature from creator. Instead they profess a monistic belief in the presence of divinity in everything in different degrees.[9] These beliefs are long-standing and pervasive throughout South Asia. Daripallans are aware of the Hindu claims, but they dispute their validity. Allah is One and Almighty, and no man, not even the Prophet Muhammad, shares in his divinity. Creation out of any substance renders the creature absolutely distinct from Allah. Adam was the result of Allah's creative power, but he did not share that power or divinity in any way.

Furthermore, Adam's creation from earth distinguished him from all of Allah's other creatures. In particular, Adam, the creature of earth, was different than the Prophet Muhammad, Allah's creature of light. It must be stressed that the farmers of Daripalla do not attribute divinity to Muhammad because of the substance from which he was created, or because of the priority of his creation. The Prophet Muhammad is only a creature, albeit a special one. Daripallans clearly distinguish themselves from Christians whom they are aware attribute divinity to the man · Jesus. Although the Prophet is very special, he is in no way divine. To attribute divinity to any creature is the greatest and most obvious of errors. However, the Prophet is special; he is not like the rest of men, although he too was a man. Because of Muhammad's precedence as a creature of Allah's light, he became Allah's final messenger, his Prophet, and he revealed the final and complete dispensation of Allah's law to men in the Quran and in his own teachings, or the Traditions. Light gave the Prophet Muhammad the special place and power to be Allah's messenger. A few Daripallans elaborate further upon the characteristics of Muhammad's nature, but for most of these farmers the recognition of the distinction between Muhammad and Adam is sufficient.

Although Adam was a lesser creation of Allah than Muhammad, he was created superior to Iblis, Allah's creature of fire. A great deal of the emphasis in the creation story is placed upon the disctinction between earth and fire with the intention of establishing the superiority of earth to fire. Daripallan farmers are most interested in the properties and powers associated with the earth as a result of this emphasis. Fire as a substance with particular powers and properties which give their particular characteristics to Iblis and the other angels is of little interest to Daripallns. To know that they are superior to these creatures, as well as to jinn and ghosts who also share in the illusiveness of fire, is sufficient for them. However, there are good historical reasons for this emphasis on the contrast between earth and fire in the creation story. Islam was brought to Bengal by Sufi mystics or saints who were missionary preachers. Islam appeared as an alternative to Hindu beliefs about the nature of reality which posited a pervasive, though graded, divinity within all of the visible and invisible substances and beings of the world.[10] Fire was an important substance associated with divinity in the Hindu world view. For the Muslim preachers to make fire interior to earth was to posit a radically different world view. Although this polemic is not part of the common perceptions among Daripallans, it has had its effects upon them. This is most clearly obvious in the elaboration of positive meanings attributed to earth among these farmers.

Because Adam and his descendants in Daripalla are creatures of earth, they are different than Allah, Muhammad, Iblis, as well as the rest of Allah's creatures. These negative associations are all directly attributable to the substance earth. However, earth also carries positive meanings for Daripallans which are central to their ethos and world view. The most significant complex of meaning associated with earth is that which has to do with the interrelated concepts of physical strength (sakti), ability, talent, dynamism (khamata), and mastery or authority (adhikar). In the creation story Adam is said to be talented (khamatasali) because he was created from the earth. Implicit in this attribution is the concept of physical strength (sakti). Further, because he was talented, Allah declared him the master (malik = owner, possessor) of the earth. Implicit in this declaration for Daripallans is the concept of mastery or authority (adhikar). To summarize these concepts, because he was created from earth, Adam possessed physical strength (sakti), talent and dynamism (khamata), and he was made master or possessor (malik) of the earth. As the earth's first malik, he had complete mastery or authority (adhikar) over the earth.

For Daripallans Adam's physical strength was the immediate and most obvious result of the earthiness of his creation. A homologous relationship is seen as existing between the earth, the food it produced for Adam's consumption, and human physical strength (sakti).[11] Power and strength are inherent in the earth. Certain fields produce better crops, certain fields produce crops that are full of more sakti or "vitamins" than others. A field full of strong dirt produces powerful food which can be converted into bodily strength (sakti, deherbol, jor) by eating it. A well-fed person can perform all his tasks properly. He has the strength to make the needed decisions, and to perform the physical labor accompanying the decisions.

For Daripallans the ability or capacity (khamata) to make ordinary, as well as important, decisions is directly linked to the earth. Adam displayed this capacity by "learning the names" of Allah's creatures. To know the name of something in Bengali is to comprehend its nature or purpose, and therefore, to be able to interrelate with it. Adam's homologous relationship with the earth was the source of this internal capacity on his part. Unlike dualistic Western thought, Daripallans do not distinguish body from mind, or the physical from the spiritual in man. Rather, man is a monistic whole created from the earth and dependent upon the earth. Adam was the first such creature, but all his descendants are too. As a result of their monistic conceptions of man and because of the homologous relationship man has with the earth, a proper diet is very significant for Daripallans. A person's diet of properly power-filled food produces not only physical strength and stamina, but at the same time it produces a man's talent, ability and dynamism. In Daripalla a farmer can most skillfully make use of his land when he is well-fed. He is best at handling the intricacies of being in charge of and responsible for his family (pari-bar), when his land produces abundantly for his consumption. When a farmer possesses a great deal of food-producing land, he is also considered capable of being active in public affairs which transcend his own family interests. He can be a "big man" (baralok) in his local community.[12] Further, only the well-fed person is considered capable of studying successfully. Food from the earth produces not only the stamina necessary to compete in the system of school examinations, but this food also produces the necessary ability. Furthermore, the earth in each particular area of Bangladesh has its own characteristics, and produces its own variations in ability (khamata). This is considered most obvious in the case of the local versions of Bengali spoken in different regions of Bangladesh. Only by eating the food produced from the land in Daripalla itself is it possible to learn their particular version of Bengali, which Daripallans refer to as their mother tongue. Food produces not only strength, but it also produces ability. By eating, a person transforms the power and strength, the "vitamins," in the food simultaneously into bodily strength and personal ability. Sakti and khamata must be separated in order to discuss them, but for Daripallans sakti/khamata are together aspects of only one reality, the reality of being a creature made from earth and sustained by the earth, a descendant of Adam.

Being a creature made from the earth and sustained by it, a strong and talented creature, Adam was particularly well-suited to be master (malik) of the earth. Allah declared that Adam was to possess the earth and be in control of the earth. This would have occured even without Adam's disobedience in heaven in eating the plant Allah had forbidden him. Being placed on earth was not inherently part of Adam and Howa's punishment for their disobedience. That they began to urinate and defecate, on the other hand, was an inherent punishment that fit the crime. This development made it impossible for them to remain in heaven any longer. Allah punished Adam and Howa further by placing them down on earth at a considerable distance from each other. They spent a considerable period of time searching for each other before they were reunited in Mecca. Although Adam took up his appointed task as the master of the earth under adverse circumstances, it was for this that he was uniquely suited. As the master of the earth, Adam possessed the power, authority, or mastery (adhikar) to make whatever decisions were necessary to productively use the earth. Implicit in the concept of having mastery over the earth is the understanding that the earth is to be cultivated and food produced. Adam was not established as a landlord, or as a speculator in property, or as an entrepeneur in the raw materials of the earth. Adam was given the sole right to decide what land was to be cultivated, when it was to be cultivated, how it was to be farmed, and how often it was to be used. From the fruits of this endeavor Adam was to nourish himself and Howa, and together they were to produce sons and daughters who would carry on in Adam's role as master of the earth and in Howa's role as wife and mother.

Down through history Adam's descendants are considered to have continued in control of the earth. Unlike Adam who controlled the whole earth, however, his ever increasing number of descendants have been themselves masters (malik) over smaller and smaller shares of land. Nevertheless, that they possess any share of land at all allows Adam's descendants to share in the mastery (adhikar) first bestowed upon Adam by Allah. Those males in Daripalla who possess land are considered to be malik. A person may possess many things: books, bicycles, clothes and so on, but only the person who possesses land is a malik in the fullest sense, as Adam was. The usual way for a person to come into possession of land is through its inheritance from his father. Occasionally, a man will be able to purchase land, or may gain the use of land through his wife's inheritance from her father. No matter how possession or control of land occurs, a person is then a malik who has mastery (adhikar) over that land. The amount of land a person has mastery over is also important in Daripalla. The more land a malik possesses, the more masterful is he considered to be. Because of the homologous relationship that exists between earth, food, strength and talent (sakti/khamata), a malik who has more food-producing land than someone else potentially has more power than that other person. If he productively cultivates this land, he will have more and better food from which he derives more strength and talent than the lesser land-holder. The organization of power and authority in Daripalla in all its complexity[13] is seen as ultimately stemming from the possession of earth, out of which Adam was created.

Concommitant upon the possession of land is a person's position as the master or malik of his own family (paribar). Neither marriage nor the birth of children is considered sufficient to make a male Daripallan the master (in American usage, the "head") of his own family. As a matter of course, sons are usually married while their father is still alive. These sons continue to reside with their wives in their father's home, and they are considered to be part of their father's paribar or family. In so far as soons and their wives and children are dependent (paribar means "dependents") upon their father for food, they are subject to his authority or mastery. In fact, anyone who regularly accepts his daily cooked food from a malik is considered part of that malik's family. Only when a son becomes the possessor land in his own right, does he become the master of his own family. Only a malik can use the Bengali phrase "my family" (amar paribar); all other members of this unit and outsiders refer to this paribar as that of its particular malik. The mastery that the malik of a family possesses is considered to be part of his fundamental composition, part of his nature. When a person becomes a malik through inheritance or purchase of land, he is said to take control over that land by "eating" it. His mastery is likewise described as something that has become an integral part of himself because he has consumed it (antarbhukta). As long as he possesses land which produces his own food, and food to give to his family, the malik remains a masterful (adhikari) person, and he remains the only masterful person within the family. The image of the malik which is maintained among Daripallans is that of Adam created as a single, autonomous creature, from whose own body Allah created his wife Howa as another autonomous but dependent creature. Together with her Adam produced all his sons and daughters. A malik in Daripalla possesses the earth and is sustained by it. Together with his wife he has produced his family. Through his own efforts and with the help of his wife and children he maintains his family in as happy and satisfied a state as possible. This is what the malik's own father did before him, and what Adam had done originally.

CONCLUSION

The creation story as a whole and the symbol of earth in particular are extrinsic, non-genetic sources of information for the farmers of Daripalla. They are cultural sources of information which are at the same time models of perceived reality and models for the perception of reality.[14] As models of reality they are formulated and developed in terms of that very reality being modeled. It is impossible to perceive the significance of earth in the creation story without being made aware of earth's utilitarian significance and properties for Daripallans. However, the creation story and the earth as symbolic also provide models for life in Daripalla. The symbol earth with its associated complex of meanings directly influences the structure of this lived-in reality which is being modeled. The authoritarian structure of family life around the malik upon whom the members are dependent is directly influenced by the creation story and the earth. Community activity in Daripalla engaged in by the most masterful of malik, the "big men," is also influenced by their possession of earth. In particular, the life of the individual malik is directly affected by the modeling activity provided by his symbols.

A common pasttime for a malik in Daripalla is to visit each of his fields which may be scattered over a fairly wide area of the country-side. An idiomatic expression is used to refer to this activity, matite yaoya, which translates literally as "going to (the) earth." A Daripallan farmer takes great pleasure in examining the progress of the corps in each of his fields, checking the conditions of the moisture in the earth, examining its need for fertilizer and possibly even insecticide. He remembers past success and failure, and he plans the future use of these fields. He makes no secret of his desire to acquire other fields. As the idiomatic expression for this activity indicates, the earth (mati) is the focus of his attention. He goes out to examine it because he draws his sustenance, his strength and talent, and his mastery from this earth. The earth not only stands for or represents to him the various meanings which he associates with it, but the earth actually effects for him these realities. Farming the earth is not simply a utilitarian occupation for such a farmer, but it is the activity by means of which he actualizes who he is. By possessing and farming the earth he reproduces Adam in himself. The earth is both symbol and sacrament for him.[15]

NOTES

1. Daripalla is a pseudonym for one rural Union Council ward in one Police Station of Pabna District, Bangladesh. This ward covers approximately three square miles, and has a population of slightly more than 4000 persons who live in 10 separate villages. The research upon which this paper is based was conducted between October, 1975 and October, 1976. This research was funded by a grant from Caritas-Bangladesh, a voluntary development agency headquartered in Dacca, Bangladesh. For further ethnographic detail, see my Power among the Farmers of Daripalla: A Bangladesh Village Study. (Dacca, Bangladesh: Caritas-Bangladesh, 1978).

2. Clifford Geertz, The Interpretation of Cultures. (New York: Basic Books, 1973), pp. 87-125.

3. See, for example, the following Sura of the Quran: Sura 2:22-40; 15: 25-49; 23: 13-18; 32:1-12, 38:72-86.

4. I paraphrase the story in the interest of space. However, no canonical version of the story exists in Daripalla. Instead, each teller adapts the story to the particular context and point under consideration. In the farmers' own terms, my paraphrase is an acceptable statement of the story meant to serve the purpose of this paper. For greater detail about this story and its interpretation see my Masters of Earth: Conceptions of "Power" Among the Muslims of Rural Bangladesh, (Unpublished Ph.D. Dissertation, University of Chicago, 1978) pp. 34-53.

5. Anyone familiar with the Quranic references to creation will be aware of how major a departure from orthodox tradition it is for these Bengali Muslims to make the Prophet Muhammad the first of Allah's creations.

6. For the farmers of Daripalla Islam's prophetic tradition culminates in Muhammad. However, prior to his appearance they believe a long series of named and unnamed prophets enlightened Adam's descendants about Allah's commands. These farmers consider themselves to be particularly fortunate to have access to the teachings of the Prophet Muhammad. Allah's Law (sunna) is contained in the Quran and the Prophet's Traditions.

7. Clifford Geertz, op.cit., p. 89.

8. Ibid., p. 91.

9. McKim Marriott and Ronald Inden, "An Ethnosociology of South Asian Caste Systems," A paper read at the American Anthropological Association Meetings, Toronto, December, 1972.

10. Susan Wadley, Shakti: Power in the Conceptual Structure of Karimpur Religion (Chicago: Department of Anthropology, University of Chicago, 1975), pp. 54-57.

11. This is a very limited meaning for sakti when it is contrasted with the Hindu meaning for this term. Compare Wadley, op.cit., pp. 181-188.

12. John P. Thorp, op.cit., pp. 79-118.

13. Ibid., pp. 200-219.

14. Clifford Geertz, op.cit., pp. 93-94.

15. The theoretical relationship between "symbol" and "sacrament" will be examined in an article currently in preparation that is based upon an unpublished paper of mine, "The Social and Political Significance of Food Transactions among the Hindus and Muslims of South Asia," A paper presented to the Anthropology Faculty at the University of Chicago, December, 1974. Basically, a sacrament is a symbol which is believed to effect what it signifies.

CHAPTER THREE

"Master Symbols and Cultural Codes: A Geertzian
Textual Analysis,"

James Preston
SUNY—College of Oneonta

ABSTRACT

This paper explores the impact of Geertz's work on the anthropology of religion. Special attention is given to the problem of extending Geertzian textual analysis to religions in complex civilizations. Several suggestions are proposed as preliminary steps necessary for the development of a comprehensive theory of religion growing out of the symbolic approach developed by Geertz and others.

The anthropological study of religion was once a thriving enterprise. Every respectable social scientist in the late nineteenth century devoted a substantial portion of his work to speculations about the evolution and origin of religion. In the early twentieth century the advent of fieldwork resulted in numerous limited, though substantial contributions to our understanding of religious systems in specific cultural contexts. Among American anthropologists from the Boasian school the watchword during this period was "caution." Still, important contributions were made on special topics like sacrific, taboo, magic, and witchcraft. New insights helped to refine terminology and served to either confirm or refine speculations first advanced in the nineteenth century. By the mid-twentieth century theoretical work on religion dwindled to a critical point. Levi-Strauss responded to this lack of interest in religion in 1963 when he wrote, "It seems that during the past twenty years anthropology has increasingly turned from studies in the field of religion."[1]

This comment may not have been entirely warranted. Anthony F. C. Wallace, for instance, contributed his major work on revitalization movements during this period.[2] Nevertheless, Levi-Strauss is correct in asserting that there was a general decline in the anthropological study of religion during the mid-twentieth century. The late 1960s and early 1970s, however, mark a turning point. The new symbolic school emerges with full force at this time, partially influenced by theoretical advances in linguistics and increased popular interest in religion outside of academia. Three giant figures in the anthropology of religion become prominent; these are

Claude Levi-Strauss, Victor Turner, and Clifford Geertz, each with a different approach to symbolism, but all working toward the development of a larger, more comprehensive and workable symbolic framework for the analysis of religion. And there are no signs that religion is any less vital as a topic of inquiry today. Indeed, recent refinements of terminology in the symbolic approach to religion suggests that the field remains vibrant.[3]

One of the most seminal thinkers in the symbolic study of religion is Clifford Geertz. His famous definition of religion has inspired considerable thought about the articulation of religious and cultural systems. Though he has not constructed a comprehensive theoretical framework of his own,[4] the extensive work of Geertz on symbolism will certainly play a major role in the eventual development of such a theory. His humanistic orientation and semantic approach to symbols is particularly significant because he insists on relating symbolic systems to social and psychological domains. No doubt Geertz would be the first to admit a paucity of adequate theory to cope with the broad spectrum of data on religion:

> There is, as yet, no well-established central trend of analysis, no central figure around whom to order debate, and no readily apparent system of interconnections relating the various competing trends to one another.[5]

Since Geertz wrote this passage in 1968, he has himself become a central figure. This volume attests to the impact of his thinking on scholars in many disciplines.

In this paper I shall discuss current problems in the anthropological study of religion and certain new directions suggested by the works of Geertz. Particular stress will be given to recent work on symbolic networks, metaphors, and master symbols as encoding devices that promise access to the difficult problem of conducting anthropological research in complex world religions. The paper concludes with suggested new directions of research, building on the contributions of Geertz, by extending and refining the basic concepts he has developed during the course of his work.

Symbol Complexes

Numerous terms have been developed by symbolic anthropologists to characterize key elements of ritual and myth. Terms like "key symbols," "dominant symbols," "structure," "core symbols," "focal symbols," and "root metaphors" attempt to identify major structural components that provide access to deep levels of meaning in symbolic systems.[6] The common denominator here is an attempt to develop concepts capable of extending symbolic analysis beyond superficial reductionism. Geertz, for instance, is concerned primarily with the problem of meaning in symbolic complexes. Yet, he is always careful to relate this symbolic level of analysis to actual social, historical and psychological aspects of the larger cultural system as a whole.[7] This is the mark of his genius.

For Geertz symbols are not mere cognitive elements; they organize experience, point to conflict between good and evil,[8] and act as metasocial commentaries. Symbols do not float in space, unattached to the human condition. They are organized into networks of meaning through intricately woven symbol complexes. Religious systems are composed of clusters of sacred symbols organized into an ordered whole.[9] Here I will distinguish between three types of symbol complexes; religious, social, and cultural. Religious symbol complexes are concerned with defining notions of transcendence in the human experience. Social symbol complexes have to do with establishing and maintaining bonds between individuals and groups of individuals in particular social organizations. Cultural symbol complexes integrate human beings into a common lifestyle. These categories are not mutually exclusive. Different types of symbol complexes are interconnected; one type may substitute for another through transposition, especially under emergency conditions. (Revitalization movements, for instance, often represent the temporary collapse of social and cultural symbol systems into the religious domain.)

Symbol complexes form the fundamental building blocks of cultures. At a higher level of abstraction are civilizations, composed of cultural fragments, involving hundreds of compounded and interlocked symbol complexes. The significant ingredient that differentiates civilizations from cultures is a mechanism for establishing hierarchies of symbol complexes, maintained and often jealously guarded by an exclusive elite. Symbol complexes in civilizations become organized in multiconnected levels of meaning. These networks of interconnected symbol complexes act as umbrellas to subsume numerous divergent religious, social and cultural elements within a single unified, though heterogeneous system. All the complex phases of human life in a civilization become interpreted and reinterpreted at different levels within the system through a process of symbolic metabolism. These transformations occur within the civilization through interlinkages at local, district, regional and macro levels. This vast network of interconnected symbols arches above the infrastructure and culminates in a few "master symbols?" The function of a master symbol complex is to summarize the formula of interrelated principles governing the process as a whole.

"Master symbols" organize complexes of minor symbols into a more or less unified Great Tradition. An excellent example of a "master symbol" is the Virgin of Guadalupe in Mexico.[10] The cult of Guadalupe integrates both Indian and Spanish elements of Mexican civilization. She is portrayed as the dark-skinned (Indian) mother who suffers for her people, takes them into battle for independence, and links them into the Spanish Catholic tradition and the Roman Church through an elaborate, international pilgrimage cycle. The "master symbol" is more than a "dominant symbol" in Turner's sense, or the "core symbol" noted by Geertz. "Master symbols" are not merely dominant in a particular setting; they are closer to what Ortner calls "key symbols" because they unlock the main thematic code of a civilization, incorporating more localized dominant and subordinate or minor symbols.[11] The following scheme suggests the relationship between different magnitudes of key symbols in a civilization.

The Master Code of a Civilization
Figure 1

Master Symbol Complex

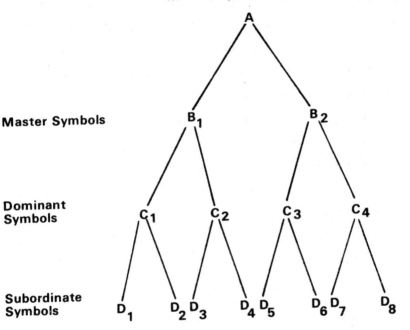

"Master symbols" must not be confused with universal symbols associated with the great world religions (such as Buddha, Christ, Virgin Mary, Shiva). Though most religious "master symbols" participate in, or borrow from, larger world-wide networks of universal symbols, they are also unique to their own cultures or civilizations. For example, it would be impossible to say anything about Mexican civilization by only studying the Virgin Mary (a universal symbol), yet an analysis of the Virgin of Guadalupe (master symbol) unlocks some of the key elements associated with the formation of Mexican national consciousness.

An important question arises as to the reasons for certain symbols to become "master symbols." Why does a particular symbol emerge into such a prominent position? Are there certain sociocultural conditions that precipitate the evolution of a "master symbol complex?" The most important qustion, however, is how "master symbols" act as agents or bearers of master codes for civilazations. At this point we have little systematic data on "master symbols." Therefore, most of these questions are difficult to answer. It does seem, however, that "master symbols" arise in the crucible of conflict, war and dissonance; that they are almost always representations of some kind of intense divine struggle between the forces of "good" and "evil"; and that they often give a sense of promise to oppressed peoples, while simultaneously offering a sense of purpose to the oppressors. Thus, "master symbols" maximize paradoxes and provide room for flexible action in the civilizational code as it amalgamates different, sometimes disparate elements into a unified whole. This process of amalgamation is illustrated in ancient Egyptian civilization where the God-King becomes fused with the "master symbols" of the Sun, monuments are then built to perpetuate the "master symbol complex," and the whole system culminates in an elaborate array of interlinked minor themes. "Master symbols" bind human beings with the cosmos in self-perpetuating systems of ordered, highly formulated social, psychological and religious patterns of meaning.

The Code

"Master symbol complexes" summarize master codes. It is in the nature of the symbol to simultaneously reveal and conceal, pointing toward another order of reality. As I. M. Lewis expresses it, "Symbolism consequently becomes a kind of sign language or semaphore, a code which is only intelligible once you have discovered the key."[12] Other terms have been employed with reference to the coded element in religious and cultural systems; namely, "model," "map," "programme," "template," "metaphor," and "root paradigm."[13] The entire school of symbolic anthropology is involved in some fashion with the problem of decoding symbol complexes.

The information locked in symbolic systems is the cultural equivalent of the genetic, biological code. Geertz expresses this homology in an eloquent passage from his famous article on religion as a cultural system:

As the order of bases in a strand of DNA forms a coded program, a set of instructions, or a recipe, for the synthesization of the structurally complex proteins which shape organic functioning, so culture patterns provide such programs for the institution of the social and psychological processes which shape public behavior. Though the sort of information and the mode of its transmission are vastly different in the two cases, this comparison of gene and symbol is more than a strained analogy of the familiar 'social heredity' sort. It is actually a substantial relationship, for it is precisely the fact that genetically programmed processes are so highly generalized in men, as compared with lower animals, that culturally programmed ones are so important, only because human behavior is so loosely determined by intrinsic sources of information that extrinsic sources are so vital. [14]

Thus, according to Geertz, cultural systems give meaning by acting as models of reality and for reality. The symbolic code is a mechanism by which human cultures adapt and participate in the creation of a reality.

Turner utilizes a similar, though different, perspective in his concept of "root paradigms." These symbolic coding devices are employed by man to organize life at increasingly more complex levels of integration:

Root paradigms are the cultural transliterations of genetic codes — they represent that in the human individual as a cultural entity which the DNA and RNA codes represent in him as a biological entity, the species life raised to the more complex and symbolic organizational level of culture. [15]

This is slightly different language to express an idea shared by Geertz, that symbolic systems are not mere epiphenomena, but have distinct and significant functions in the maintenance and perpetuation of cultural systems.

Recently other symbolic anthropologists have tried to isolate the encoding devices of cultures through the analysis of "key symbols" and "metaphors." Ortner differentiates between two types of key symbols: (1) summarizing symbols that condense complex ideas in a unitary system, and (2) elaborating symbols which are vehicles for sorting out complex ideas and feelings. [16] According to Ortner, summarizing symbols relate to the sacred domain while elaborating symbols assist people with problem solving in everyday life. Thus, symbols crystallize and integrate lower-order meanings with higher-order assumptions. The meaning of the code is enshrined in the summarizing symbol which mediates between different levels of the cultural system.

Another important contribution to understanding symbolic codes is found in a recent article by Beck. She believes that "metaphors" are the keys that " . . . unlock the secrets of the human culture-building process."[17] Beck calls our attention to both verbal and nonverbal forms of the metaphor. The essential nature of the metaphor is to juxtapose elements of a concrete image in order to formulate more abstract relationships.[18] Metaphors mediate between two modes of thought (sensory and abstract), allowing human beings to introduce nonverbal material into semantic contexts. Thus, to Beck metaphors are devices that bridge affective and cognitive domains in the human experience. The code is not completely cerebral or rational, but also has important nonverbal, analogical and emotional components.

Several scholars have criticized the French Structuralist school of thought (Levi-Strauss and Leach) for placing too much emphasis on quasi-linguistic or cognitive interpretations of symbol systems. Geertz and Lewis, for instance, accuse the French Structuralists of searching for secret cerebral messages in symbolic codes.[19] Beck adds an important additional criticism when she castigates the structuralists for seeking a single central message; symbolic codes are not that simple. They condense numerous multilevel packets of information.[20] She argues that metaphors have been overlooked by anthropologists and can help us to understand the "ultimate cosmic constructs" in cultural systems.[21]

Whether the emphasis is on "root paradigms," "key symbols," "metaphors," or "master symbols" (as I have done in this paper) no one says much about the code itself. How is it perpetuated? What are the sets of instructions in the code? Why is the code usually secret, shared by a few, yet influential for all? If public behavior is shaped by these codes, how does that happen? Perhaps most important is the danger of reading too much into a cultural code. Also, if there are clear encoding devices embedded in cultural systems, the discovery of such codes should allow for relatively accurate prediction of behavior. Unfortunately the state of the science of symbolism remains relatively undeveloped, so that most of these questions cannot be answered until further baseline research has been conducted. One important place to begin such research is in complex civilizational contexts, where symbolic systems are associated with particularly rich written and oral traditions.

Decoding a Mosaic Text

Geertz treats cultures as texts. The task of the anthrpologist is to read the cultural text of a people. The text is not to be dissected, but treated as an integral whole, a system of meaning, a metasocial commentary for sorting out human beings. Thus, a culture is an ensemble of symbolic texts, woven irreversably together, in a complex matrix of meaning.[22]

A textual approach to symbolic analysis avoids the pitfalls of dissecting the phenomenon beyond all recognition. This methodology is refreshing to students of the great world religions who find themselves overwhelmed with the deep interconnectedness of their topic of inquiry. It is no accident that Geertz conducted his major fieldwork in three civilizational contexts: Java, Bali, and Morocco. The methodology he has developed in these settings offers the anthropologist significant advantages for working in peasant societies. The interweaving of myths and rites in these civilizations is sometimes so intricate that anthropologists often become overwhelmed with the sheer task of sorting our trivial details from elements of core meaning. Turner expresses this same concern for the great intricacy of civilizations in the following passage:

> It would seem that it is principally among agriculturally based societies with deep traditions of continuous residence in a single region that one may find cultures of the signatura rerum type, where every element is interwoven with every other in a fine tapestry of symbols and ideas.[23]

It is this "tapestry of symbols" which challenges our methodology. Geertz has given us an excellent mode of access by treating them as texts; to be understood as whole systems, each part entwined with the others.

The problem is to find interconnections between various symbol clusters in a civilization. I shall use the term "mosaic text" to refer to the overall pattern of symbols found in civilizations. The reason I have selected this term is to illustrate the unique quality of what has been termed "civilization" among Western scholars. As noted earlier in this paper, civilizations are composed of fragments of many cultures that have been amalgamated in a single hierarchical system. I refer to civilizations as "mosaic texts" because of the integrity of subcultural units (subsystems or clusters of symbols) that remain more or less in tact, despite the overall process of assimilation in the system. A "mosaic text" is organized around an assemblage of quite diverse dominant symbol clusters that interlink at the highest level of integration through a "master symbol complex" (sometimes called the Great Tradition). Thus, the key to a "mosaic text" is the symbol complex where the master code is embedded. This master code carries the mechanism for assimilating and transforming subcultural elements within the system. A "mosaic text," however, never succeeds at metabolizing all sub-cultural elements into the civilizational core; for the master code at the center generates divergence as well as unity. While it reinterprets local elements of the subcultures, it simultaneously preserves much of their separate integrity.

The Hindu Mosaic

One of the most complex civilizations in the world is that vast mosaic of life styles found in the Indian subcontinent. The great diversity of symbolic systems in India almost defies anthropological analysis. Consequently, South Asian specialists have been forced to limit their studies to particular regions and localities. However, by combining Geertz' concept of "cultural text" with new methods for research on networks developed by Turner,[24] it may be possible to fathom the underlying code or set of codes within the Indian mosaic.

Perhaps one of the least developed aspects of Indian ethnography is a comprehensive study of Hinduism. Despite many excellent contributions by anthropologists over the years, considerable gaps still remain. Today there is a need to integrate earlier regional and local studies of Hinduism in order to discover the larger all-India pattern. This requires the following preparatory ethnographic baseline work: (1) a classification of Hindu temples and shrines;[25] (2) studies of pilgrimage cycles at all-India, regional, district, and local levels within the system; (3) a focus on the elaboration, distribution, and evolution of "master symbols" in the Hindu mosaic; (4) a study of the connection of these symbolic elements to social, psychological and cultural factors in the larger whole. Not until this kind of baseline work has been accomplished will it be possible to piece together the larger process, decode it, and understand the evolution of religious consciousness as it interlinks with changes in the overall civilization.

Hinduism has no clear institutional superstructure like the ecclesiastical hierarchies found in Christendom. This may be a blessing in disguise because it forces South Asian specialists to reach deeply, and probe beneath, the institutions that form the backbone of Hinduism. Nevertheless, there is always the temptation to overemphasize some regional variant of Hinduism and generalize to the whole system without accounting for different levels in the mosaic structure. Nor can a "mosaic text" be understood by segmenting it into neat binary categories largely formulated in the minds of Western scholars. Notions like Great and Little Traditions, Low and High religions, etc. are convenient heuristic devices; but more often than not they become easily reified and distort the data unnecessarily. "Mosaic texts" are not structured in binary formats. It would be virtually impossible to arrange a mosaic pattern along simple binary lines. A more useful model must be multidimensional in scope.

Cartesian dualism is perpetuated in anthropological studies of religion by the followers of Redfield (American), Levi-Strauss (French), and Turner (British). Only Geertz (and some of his followers) somehow has managed to transcend this problem. Hinduism has not been approached by anthropologists without some kind of hidden dualistic model. Yet, of all religions, Hinduism challenges, even the most superficial observer, to set aside such shallow and misleading binary thinking. South Asian ethnologists have failed to cope with the enormous textual and con- textual diversity of the subcontinent. This is partially due to a long preoccupa- tion of anthropologists with the Indian caste system. Hinduism itself has been usual- ly a topic of secondary interest.[26] Another reason for the neglect of Hinduism as a focus for research has been the difficulty of access for foreign scholars to the inner workings of temples. This poorly developed ethnography of Hinduism renders South Asian specialists incapable of piecing together a large comprehensive view of the subcontinent; for religion in general, and Hinduism specifically, forms a key ingredient in Indian civilization. Thus, the codes in the Hindu mosaic remain largely unfathomed. We are now at the brink of cracking these codes through new research presently being conducted on patterns of pilgrimage, major and minor Hindu shrines, and the religious experiences of individuals who are the receptacles of codes.

Conclusion

It is not possible in this brief space to explore all the potential ramifications of Geertz's work. I have tried to indicate here how significant the textual approach may be for better access to studies of complex civilizational religions. But there is considerable groundwork that still needs to be done. The terminology in this field remains relatively loose and sloppy. Also, the notion of "cultural codes" may be erroneous. Are we abdicating responsibility by turning to easy formulas to comprehend complex socio-cultural systems? This problem of error can only be detected when we have tested the predictability of such cultural codes in determining human behavior in specific contexts. Another important question is how one goes about decoding something as intricate as a "mosaic text."

Geertz gives us certain hints in his brilliant work on Java,[27] where the master code is embedded in each regional variant. The problem is to unlock several of these sub-codes in order to reveal the deeper, sometimes invisible master code. The mosaic is an organization of variant symbol complexes emerging out of numerous converging themes that have been woven together in consistent patterns over time. The "master symbol complex" grounds individuals into the system as a whole, despite the great divergence in the "mosaic text."[28] The whole system defies analysis unless the researcher is willing to work in a multidimensional framework. So far anthropologists have developed adequate tools to investigate social, ritual and mythic domains in a particular symbolic system, but these three levels are not sufficient to give us a full picture of the phenomenon.

To attain the depth of analysis necessary for a comprehensive study of religious and cultural codes it is necessary to penetrate beneath surface levels of meaning. Symbols are grounded in human experience. No matter how elegant our clever abstractions may be about the transmission of codes, ultimately these codes must be connected to human emotions. Several scholars, including Geertz, have castigated the Structuralist school for omitting emotional factors in their extreme cerebral interpretations of religion.[29] Yet Geertz himself has contributed little to the understanding of human affect. Indeed, few anthropologists have devoted any attention to the topic of religious experience.

The lack of understanding of religious experience is compounded with another, even more important problem in the anthropological study of religion. This is the problem of "consciousness." Many important issues about the role of culture in human adaptation are related to man's high degree of awareness and flexibility for developing adaptive strategies in the face of environmental changes. We know almost nothing about the relationship of symbols to consciousness in man. The capacity for language (the process of encoding and decoding messages) is somehow related to a fantastic elaboration of the cerebral cortex, which must in some way be accompanied by a high degree of consciousness about the world. What is the relationship of symbolic codes to human consciousness? Once again we are left with little information from fieldwork, because this aspect of human symbol making remains almost completely unexplored by anthropologists.

Geertz has laid the groundwork for a comprehensive theory of religion. His insistence that such a theory should be multidimensional and non-reductionist must be taken seriously. I have tried here to outline some preliminary steps for constructing such a theory. These include; (1) The acceptance of ontological status for symbolic behavior. (Religion is not a mere epiphenomenon.)[30] (2) The treatment of symbolic systems as texts. (3) More studies of "master symbol" complexes. (4) A better understanding of symbolic networks and their relationship to different levels of socio-cultural integration.[31] (5) Studies of religious experience, including the linkage between symbols and consciousness.

The resurgence of interest in religion among contemporary anthropologists marks a major turning point in the history of the discipline. We stand now at the threshold between an earlier emphasis on positivism and a new emphasis on humanism within the field of anthropology. This "humanistic revival" is not, for the most part, a wild and undisciplined application of intuition to social phenomena, but rather an attempt to recapture the human element that was lost by too much emphasis on methods and assumptions borrowed from the natural sciences in order to establish anthropology as a legitimate scientific enterprise. Geertz is a central figure in this humanistic revival. He combines the best of humanism and the scientific method. No other contemporary anthropologist of religion balances these two perspectives so effectively. He challenges us to reach deeply in order to understand the evolution of symbolic systems without losing the human touch.

NOTES

1. Claude Levi-Strauss, Structural Anthropology, p. 202.

2. Anthony F. C. Wallace, "Revitalization Movements," 264-281.

3. See Brenda Beck, "The Metaphor," 83-97 and Sherry Ortner, "On Key Symbols," 1338-1346.

4. Sherry Ortner, "Gods' Bodies; Gods' Food," p. 133.

5. Clifford Geertz, "Religion: Anthropological Study," p. 403.

6. Sherry Ortner, "Gods' Bodies; Gods' Food," p. 134.

7. See Clifford Geertz, "Deep Play," p. 17 and Clifford Geertz, "Religion as a Cultural System," p. 42.

8. Clifford Geertz, "Ethos, World-View and the Analysis of Sacred Symbols," p. 425.

9. Ibid, p. 424.

10. See the brilliant article by Eric Wolf "The Virgin of Guadalupe" for the evaboration of a "master symbol" in Mexico. Also see Cult of the Goddess by James Preston.

11. See Sherry Ortner, "On Key Symbols," 1338-1346.

12. I. M. Lewis, "Introduction," p. 1.

13. Sherry Ornter, "Gods' Bodies, Gods' Food," p. 133.

14. Clifford Geertz, "Religion as a Cultural System," pp. 6 & 7.

15. Victor Turner, Dramas, Fields, and Metaphors, p. 67.

16. Sherry Ortner, "On Key Symbols," p. 1340.

17. Brenda Beck, "The Metaphor," p. 83.

18. Ibid, pp. 83 & 87.

19. See Clifford Geertz, "Religion: Anthropological Study," p. 405 and I. M. Lewis, "Preface," p. vii.

20. Ibid, p. 86.

21. Brenda Beck, "The Metaphor," p. iv.

22. Clifford Geertz, "Deep Play," pp. 26 & 29.

23. Victor Turner, Dramas, Fields, and Metaphors, p. 163.

24. See Ibid pp. 166-230 and Victor Turner, Image and Pilgrimage in Christian Culture.

25. See James J. Preston, "Sacred Centers and Symbolic Networks in India."

26. There are numerous exceptions. The works of Bharati, Singer, Srinivas and Babb have contributed significantly to the understanding of Hinduism.

27. Clifford Geertz, The Religion of Java.

28. Sherry Ortner, "On Key Symbols," p. 1344.

29. Clifford Geertz, "Religion: Anthropological Study," p. 405 and I. M. Lewis, "Introduction," p. 2.

30. Victor Turner, Dramas, Fields, and Metaphors, p. 57.

31. James J. Preston, "Sacred Centers and Symbolic Networks in India."

REFERENCES CITED

Babb, Lawrence, The Divine Hierarchy. New York: Columbia University Press, 1975

Beck, Brenda. "The Metaphor: Mediator between Modes of Thought." Current Anthropology 19 (March 1978): 83-97.

Bharati, Agehananda. "Pilgrimage Sites and Indian Civilization." In Chapters in Indian Civilization, Vol. I. Edited by Joseph Elder. Dubuque, Iowa: Kendall/Hunt Publishing Co., 1970.

Geertz, Clifford. "Deep Play: Notes on the Balinese Cockfight." In Myth, Symbol and Culture, pp. 1-38. Edited by Clifford Geertz. New York: W. W. Norton & Co., 1971.

_____. "Ethos, World-View and the Analysis of Sacred Symbols." Antioch Review (December 1957): 421-437.

_____. "Religion: Anthropological Study." In International Journal of the Social Sciences, Vol. 13, pp. 398-406.

_____. "Religion as a Cultural System." In Anthropological Approaches to the Study of Religion, pp. 1-46. Edited by Michael Banton. London: Tavistock Publishers, 1966.

_____. The Religion of Java. New York: The Free Press, 1960.

Levi-Strauss, Claude. Structural Anthropology. Garden City: Doubleday and Co.,, 1963.

Lewis, I. M.: "Introduction." In Symbols and Sentiments. Edited by I. M. Lewis. London: Academic Press, 1977.

Ortner, Sherry. "Gods' Bodies, Gods' Food." In The Interpretation of Symbolism, pp. 133-169. Edited by Roy Willis. New York: John Wiley and Sons, 1975.

_____. "on Key Symbols," American Anthropologist (1973): 1338-1346.

Preston, James J. Cult of the Goddess. New Delhi: Vikas Publishers, (in press).

_____. "Sacred Centers and Symbolic Networks in India." Paper presented at the Xth International Congress of Anthropological and Ethnological Sciences, New Delhi, India, December, 1978.

Singer, Milton. When a Great Tradition Modernizes. New York: Praeger Publishers, 1972.

Srinivas, M. N. Social Change in Modern India. Berkeley: University of California Press, 1969.

Turner, Victor. Dramas, Fields, and Metaphors. Ithaca: Cornell University Press, 1974.

Turner, Victor and Turner, Edith. Image and Pilgrimage in Christian Culture. New York: Columbia University Press, 1978.

Wallace, Anthony F. C. "Revitalization Movements." American Anthropologist 45 (1943): 230-240.

Wolf, Eric. "The Virgin of Guadalupe: A Mexican National Symbol." Journal of American Folklore 71 (1958): 34-39.

CHAPTER FOUR

"The Siona Hallucinogenic Ritual: It's Meaning and Power"

E. Jean Langdon
Cedar Crest College

ABSTRACT

Using Geertz's definition of religion, the paper explores the hallucinogenic ritual of the Siona Indians as a dramatic symbolic presentation of the key conceptions of Siona world view. It also analyzes the use of hallucinogens as a powerful method fusing the imagined and common-sense realities and deeply affecting daily life and · behavior.

"Beware of snakes and piranha," I was warned by well meaning relatives and friends as I set off to live with the Siona Indians of the Amazon Basin. Arriving there, I received an entirely different set of warnings, "Don't go out at night, the spirits are out; don't go near the silk cotton tree or you will get ill; don't go in that clearing in the jungle, for those spirits don't like women." I found that the Siona live with feelings of awe and fear of the jungle, but that their fears do not correspond with mine at all. I feared getting lost, lacking the knowledge of the jungle paths. They feared being captured by the spirits, which cause them to get lost. I feared snakes. They feared the shaman who sent the snake to bit. I feared the jaguars; they feared the shamans who were jaguars. I feared the strength of the river current and the electric eels. They feared the river people who eat your soul and cause illness. Our conceptions of the order of the world differed radically, and we travelled in very different jungles that were colored by our different perceptions.

In this paper I shall explore the process by which the Siona conception of order works to color every day life. Clifford Geertz's model of religion as a cultural system will be used.[2] His definition of religion provides a useful way of looking at Siona religion, for it focuses upon religion as a symbolic system and the way in which the symbolic system fuses religious conceptions and everyday life. Three aspects of Geertz's formulation will be explored here. First, the key conceptions that formulate Siona cosmic order will be outlined. Second, their hallucinogenic rituals will be examined in an effort to delineate how the ritual utilizes symbolic vehicles of this world view in particularly powerful ways to unite the imagined and common sense realities. Finally, the paper will examine how deeply these conceptions go in providing a template for action in the secular world. Religion pervades all aspects of the Siona's lives, and it is hoped that this study of the hallucinogenic ritual may give particular insight into the nature of its power in their lives.

Religion as a Cultural System:

As defined by Geertz, " . . . a religion is:

> (1) a system of symbols which acts to (2) establish powerful pervasive, and long-lasting moods and motivations in men by (3) formulating conceptions of a general order of existence and (4) clothing these conceptions with such an aura of factuality that (5) the moods and motivations seem uniquely realistic.[3]

This definition of religion holds within it the double aspect of religion that accounts for its power in human life. It is both a model of reality and a model for reality. On the one hand, religion is an attempt to "conserve the fund of general meanings in terms of which each individual interprets his experiences and organizes his conduct."[4] These meanings are stored in symbols and "are felt somehow to sum up, for those for whom they are resonant, what is known about the way the world is, the quality of the emotional life it supports, and the way one ought to behave while in it."[5] We find in religion a cluster of symbols that are woven into an ordered whole. This cluster formulates the general order of existence for a culture. On the other hand, the conceptions of the universe conveyed by this symbolic system are given a strong sense of reality. Powerful and pervasive moods and motivations are induced in men and guide their activities in the world. Thus, religion shapes reality as well as provides a model of it. The model of reality it presents appears so real that it is used for a plan of action.

Ritual plays a key role in religion's ability to create the "aura of factuality." It motivates men to behave as if the conceptions of general order are the true reality both within religious and secular behavior. In ritual, the world as it is imagined and the world as it is lived become fused in one set of symbolic forms. Both the dispositional and conceptual aspects of religious life converge for the believer in a "cultural performance." This convergence of ethos and world view in the ritual provides the authoritative experience which justifies the conceptual order and induces one to behave accordingly. The "moods and motivations induced by religious practice seem themselves supremely practical, the only sensible ones to adopt, given the way things 'really' are."[6] Thus, the individual leaves the ritual and returns to the common sense world changed by the experience, and in turn, the common sense world is changed.

The Imagined World:

The Siona Indians live in the dense rain forests of the Northwest Amazon Basin. Most of their settlements are scattered along large tributaries of the Amazon River in Southern Colombia and Northern Ecuador, including the Putumayo and the Aguarico Rivers. Although the recent development of oil resources has greatly influenced the group along the Putumayo, the Siona way of life has not disappeared. Men still hunt and fish for their major source of protein. Both sexes carry on slash and burn agriculture, growing traditional crops for home consumption as well as new cash crops. In particular, the Siona continue to orient to a universe whose formulation of order has been carried down from their ancestors.

The Siona often describe their universe as being composed of two sides. One side, called "this side," is the reality that we all perceive through our ordinary senses: the people, their gardens, homes, animals, and plants; the river and its fish; and the jungle and its animals. "The other side" is one of the supernatural forces and realms that cannot be seen by ordinary men and women. It consists of a world of five ascending levels, each one inhabited by various classes of supernatural beings. There is a replication on each level, for all the beings live a life similar to that which we see in "this side." The beings or spirits have houses, clothing, foods, furniture, and utensils similar to those of the Siona. The Siona believe that their own customs and material goods have been copies from their spirits. Some of them live in clan-like groups, consisting of the head spirit and his followers. The Sun is surrounded by red dancing women and young men who help guide his motor canoe that travels across the sky river every day. The Thunder Being has people who beat his drums and drink chicha, the native beer, with him. On this side, when it thunders and rains, the Siona know that they are partying with their drums and <u>chicha</u>. The thunder we hear is the beating of their drums and the rain is the <u>chicha</u> that they are spilling.

The other side of reality is of fundamental interest to the Siona, for all aspects of existence in ordinary reality are influenced by these forces and their activities. Every location, plant, and animal has a corresponding spirit in the "other side," and the activities of the spirits affect the events in this side. The supernatural forces cause the world and man to function normally. They determine good weather and the changing of the seasons for crops, the appearance of game animals for hunters to shoot, and the proper growth process expected of humans. They may also disrupt the normal routine and present dangers to the security of life. Disruptions generally occur as physical sickness, but they may be the occurrence of other dangerous abnormalities, such as food scarcities, deviant behavior, floods, and earthquakes. Hence, to live and prosper in this world, to ensure one's security, and to counteract dangers, it is necessary to learn how to live with and influence these ultimate forces. The shamans are the individuals with the knowledge and ability to enter at will the other side and to deal with the beings there. They have gained the knowledge and power to do so through frequent controlled ingestion of the hallucinogen <u>Banisteriopsis</u>, called uko in Siona, and widely known in ethnographical works as <u>yage</u> or <u>ayahuasca</u>.[7]

Traditionally the shaman is both a religious and political leader, although on the Putumayo there is no longer anyone considered knowledgeable enough or willing to assume the role. As the religious leader, the shaman leads the communal hallucinogenic rituals that are held weekly. Under his direction the community members ingest the hallucinogenic brew. Through songs and chants he guides their visionary journeys in the other side. The shaman also contacts the master spirits of the animals in order that the hunters may find game and influences the spirits of the seasons so that harvests will be abundant. During these sessions, the shaman is believed to see into the past and future, to ward off disease-causing spirits, or to cure afflicted community members. Diagnosis and cure require that the supernatural force or being be known; who, if anyone, sent the force through sorcery; and the removal of the intruded object left by the force that it may be sent back to its place of origination.

Key Symbolic Conceptions:

Geertz adopts Langer's definition of symbols when he speaks of religion as a system of symbols. A symbol is "any object, act, event, quality, or relation which serves as a vehicle for a conception — the conception is the symbol's meaning."[8] Within the Siona world view, four terms sum up the major conceptions of the Siona's universe and how the Siona hope to relate to its order. These terms, wahu, dau, ?uko, and hun?i, are not easily translated into equivalent terms. The total meaning of each one encompasses an important and general conception of their world view. By exploring the different uses and concrete representations of these terms, we shall be able to gain an understanding of these general conceptions. In this exploration we will also discover the Siona's dispositions toward them.

The first term, wahu, sums up their concern with the well being of their life and the desire to maintain health. When a Siona greets another in the traditional manner, he inquires "Are you wahu?" When translating this into Spanish, they say it means "Are you fully living?" If well, the reply is "I am wahu," or "I am living." The Siona also describe a fat person as wahu, and the quality of fatness symbolizes good health. This kind of fatness is epitomized in the plumpness of healthy babies, who are just beginning this process of living. Wahu is also used as an adjective to describe unripe plants, immature animals and people, and living objects or beings that are fresh, young, or tender. It is also used to mean light shades of the color green, such as those we might associate with spring. By examining all these meanings, there emerges a concept of what the Siona consider to be the desirable state of wahu. It implies a dynamic state of youth with the plumpness and promise of further growth. This concept is made concrete in their daily lives through the objects and people that exhibit the different qualities associated with wahu. They strive to maintain the state of wahu through the weekly hallucinogenic rituals and daily rituals performed to help them be fat, young, and healthy.

If the individual is sick, he will reply to the traditional greeting "I am hun?i" or "I am dying." Hun?i is the opposite state of wahu, and one is considered to be either in the state of growing or dying. Dying, like living, is a dynamic state for the Siona and not the short act preceding death that it is for us. For all the qualities associated with wahu, there are opposite qualities that imply the conception of the dying force in the universe. Unlike wahu, however, these qualities are not subsumed under a general term, but are expressed in various terms. Qualities associated with the state of dying include emaciation or thinness, darkness, and rottenness. These are symbolized in visions and dreams by black or rotten objects, wet or dirty clothing, or very thin spirits. The most common descriptions of poor health include references to the individual's loss of weight. Old age is also associated with being thin, when the dying forces of life are gathering strength over the living. One is past the peak of growth and now becoming old and skinny.

Examining the associations with these two conceptions represented by the terms wahu and hun?i, we can see that wahu is associated with the waxing forces of life, those that express good health and growth. The conception of dying is associated with the waning forces, those of aging and sickness. In their formulation of the cosmos, the Siona envision a life in which one or the other of the forces predominates, depending upon the disposition of the supernatural forces and the shaman's ability to control them.

?Uko is an important element in influencing the balance between those two states. When the Siona wish to contact the supernatural agents that give life and power to this reality, they gather with a shaman to ingest ?uko, the hallucinogenic brew. Both the vine and the drink are known as ?uko, as well as a very large number of plants, animals, insects, and their preparations. These latter kinds of ?uko are not intended for visions and their names consist of ?uko and an additional term that specifies the substances' use or purpose. Thus, there is cough ?uko for curing a cough, getting fat ?uko for gaining weight, and hunting ?uko for success in hunting. The hallucinogen, simply called ?uko, represents the fundamental and most general conception of the term. The specific classes are believed to derive their meaning, use, and power from this prime ?uko.

The general meaning of the term corresponds to our term "medicine," although its use indicates a meaning far more general than our connotation of the term. Its medicinal quality applies to the whole cosmic order as well as to the social order and one's bodily health. This is reflected in the two major classes of ?uko, those that produce visions and those that do not.

The ?uko that produces visions is used for its power in enabling the shaman and others to enter into the other side of reality to see what is really happening. It is essential to maintain the state of wahu and to prevent danger or disruption of normalcy by allowing the shamans to know and influence the ultimate forces behind events in this world. As we will see in our discussion of dau, ?uko, is responsible for imparting knowledge and power to the shaman which allow him to bargain with the spirits. It is also responsible for the more specific powers of the non-visionary medicines, for it is said that all other ?uko were first discovered during hallucinogenic visions. The Siona recognize and occasionally use other hallucinogenic substances, but <u>Banisteriopsis</u> is considered by them to be the fundamental medicine.

The non-visionary medicines are expected to relieve physical symptoms or to alter physiological states of man, plants, or animals. Like the vision producing medicine, this group is employed to maintain well being in all aspects of life. For example, during birth and puberty rituals specific ?uko are employed to ensure that the person will perform his or her tasks and develop properly. Medicines are applied to animals and fields. Dogs are given medicine to enable them to smell the game better. Manioc digging sticks are rubbed with medicine so the crop will be large. Medicines are applied to hunters and babies to defend them against malevolent spirits. The majority of non-visionary medicines are used to prevent or combat illness. Depending on the seriousness of the illness, these medicines may or may not be employed in conjunction with a hallucinogenic ritual. They are used in pragmatic ways, and their benefits are judged by the practical results they yield.

While hallucinogenic medicines can only be administered to others by a master shaman, this is not true of the other class. All Siona, male and female, know many herbs and other substances employed as medicines. Within the community some individuals are believed to have more knowledge than others and are consulted when no one in the immediate family knows the proper herbs. However, there is no one, professional herbalist. Advice and help in obtaining herbs is given free. Although anyone with the knowledge can administer the medicines, it is considered desirable for the shaman to chant over them in order to impart some of his curing power that he has gained from the hallucinogenic ?uko. Also, if the illness is very serious, a supernatural cause is suspected and it is deemed imperative that the hallucinogenic ritual is performed before the other medicines can restore the person to total health. Thus, although one use of medicine relates to the prevention and curing of illness in a pragmatic sense, a fundamental aspect of the conception of ?uko has to do with the power it gives to an individual to see into the unknown and to understand the true reality behind events. Seeing this reality is essential for the maintainance of a state of well being.

The final and perhaps most difficult concept to define is associated with the term dau. In response to the traditional inquiry about one's health, a Siona may reply, "I am dying from a dau," indicating that he or she is feeling ill. Dau cannot be translated simply as sickness, for its meaning is far more complex. We will explore three different meanings: 1. dau as the shaman's knowledge and power which may be embodied as a substance that grows within the shaman's body; 2. dau as a concrete witchcraft substance; and 3. dau as a sickness substance, causing a bodily ailment similar to our own colloquial meaning of "illness." In each of these cases, dau is a concrete thing existing independently of the individual rather than as an inherent quality or function of the individual.

When a man begins to drink the hallucinogen, it is said that a substance begins to grow inside him. This substance, called dau, embodies the knowledge and power that he is gaining from his experiences with the visions. The master shaman has a large amount of dau which enables him to travel to the different realms of reality in order to contact and influence the spirits; it gives him power to cure or to cause misfortune to others. The shaman derives from it the ability to induce visionary states with lesser stimulants or curing powers from the state of sweating. Without dau, he is "only a man." Non-shamans with lesser portions of dau are also able to leave their bodies and travel to spirit realms in the other side. However, since they do not possess as much knowledge and experience, they cannot travel as far as the shaman, nor do they have the power to bargain with the spirits there.

Dau is said to be dispersed throughout the shaman's body, not residing in one particular location nor having a particular form. When it leaves the body, it takes a particular form, most commonly that of a dart, a stone, or a snake's tooth. Other forms include a "rotting substance" or a "black butterfly." When a shaman teaches an apprentice his visions and songs, he imparts some of his dau to the apprentice. In these instances where the dau leaves the body, it is not implied by the Siona that the actual quantity of dau which the shaman possesses is decreased. In the abstract sense, dau is imparted as one imparts knowledge. This act is made concrete by the symbolic objects of dau that may be found outside his body. Although imparting his dau does not weaken the shaman's own quantity of dau, the novice may eventually become more powerful than his teacher and damage his dau. If the shaman fears that this may happen, it is said that he will destroy the dau that he has given by causing bad visions for the novice.

During his apprenticeship, the novice accumulates dau in his body as he continues to ingest ?uko and to travel in the visionary realms that the master shaman is showing him. As dau grows, the recipient must be ever alert to protect himself against influences that could damage it. Dau is very sensitive and vulnerable. It can be easily damaged, which results in the loss of the man's power to use his knowledge. For this reason, the Siona employ the term "delicate" to indicate that a man has begun to see the visions and accumulate dau. He is beginning to build his power and knowledge, but he must protect himself from the dangers of damage to the power. Dau may be damaged through contamination from a polluted person or from sorcery. In both cases the general result is a frightening visionary experience while intoxicated with the hallucinogenic drug, followed by illness. The curing shaman must remove the dau from the victim if he is to recover. Such a cure implies that the individual has last his knowledge.

When the Siona speak of dau inside the shaman's body, they are speaking of it in an abstract sense, as a symbol of his knowledge, as well as in the concrete sense where it is a physical substance that makes the body "delicate." When referring to dau as a witchcraft substance, the same two levels of abstractness and concreteness apply. In the abstract sense, dau is the knowledge that gives the shaman the ability to contact the spirits for beneficial purposes and also that which gives him the power to do the opposite, to cause harm. Thus, when the shaman "thinks ugly" of someone, it is the dau within him that causes misfortune to an individual. The dau has an existence somewhat independent of the action of its possessor. It is only partially under conscious control and can cause harm without the shaman actually intending his angry thoughts to take form. This is the doubled edged aspect of dau which makes its possessor so respected and feared. Dau empowers him to cure and influence forces for the best; it also gives him the ability to cause harm, either consciously or unconsciously. The shaman fights against evil, but he is also evil itself.

When speaking about dau in the concrete sense of a witchcraft object, the Siona refer to it as a physical object which may be inside the shaman, flying toward the victim, or in the victim. When inside the shaman, the dau appears in the form of darts like those of the blowgun. The forearm of the shaman serves as the "dart holder," and the darts are shot at the victim through his middle finger. When he prepares a witchcraft weapon from the dau dispersed in his body, the Siona express it as "working" or "weaving" the dau. He works it and throws it at the intended victim. If the victim is to be cured, the dau must be removed by a shaman in a hallucinogenic ritual.

The third meaning of dau is sickness. Used in this way, dau does not necessarily refer to the sorcery substance inside the individual that is causing the condition, but may be referring to the general condition of sickness in the same way that we "have" a sickness. Thus, dau does not always imply sorcery or other supernatural causation but is used in a looser metaphorical sense to imply illness. It does, however, contain the element of anxiety associated with sorcery, and if the condition persists, the term will be used to refer specifically to a suspected sorcery substance and a shaman will be called upon to confirm the suspicion through his contact with the spirit world during a hallucinogenic ritual.

I do not wish to imply that the three meanings of dau are totally distinct in the minds of the Siona. Perhaps it is more correct to say that the various uses of the term function as symbolic qualities and objects that refer to an important general conception of energy or power. The conception lying within the meanings of dau implies the potential energy source which powers the dynamic states of being, living and dying. It is manifested symbolically as a concrete presence in the shaman and activated by ?uko, or as a dau in the sense of a specific illness or illness agent. The manner in which it becomes manifest and operative depends upon various circumstantial factors, such as the knowledge, experience, and intentions of the shamans, the intentions of the spirits, and the compliance or non-compliance with mores involving pollution and purity.

The Ritual:

Let us now turn to the Siona ritual and examine the fusion of the two sides of reality through symbols and the moods and motivations produced by them. For us, it consists of a series of antics, such as dancing, singing, whistling, growling like a jaguar, climbing the rafters, and so forth. These activities are dramatically performed by the shaman, with the community members actively participating through the visions they are seeing and through singing in response to his songs. For the Siona under the effects of the hallucinogen, what happens on this side is only symbolic of what is really happening on the other side. The ritual is the visionary reality. It is experienced with all the aura of factuality that one can have in an experience. For instance, when a novice begins to drink Banisteriopsis for the first time, he has a vision in which he faces death, becomes a child, is swaddled by the Jaguar Mother, and then is thrown out by her. It is a powerful vision and is considered necessary to have it in order to leave your body. The Siona say that when the Jaguar Mother throws them out, they are seen in this side as falling from their hammocks. Onlookers know what is happening in the other side when they witness this.

Both men and women not in a state of pollution may take part in the event. The ritual is of concern and importance to the entire community, including those who will not participate, since its purpose is for the general good. Any community member's actions may affect it if he or she fails to observe a taboo, thus causing an evil spirit to "damage" the ?uko infusion, rendering the medicine dangerous for those who drink it. While the drug is being prepared on the day of the ritual, the entire community observes the taboos necessary to avoid the intrusion of evil spirits. No one bathes in the river past the noon hour; hunters stay at home; and dogs are tied up to prevent their wandering into the jungle, possibly attracting spirits. Those who plan to participate in the ceremony fast and take emetics to purge their bodies of polluting substances so that they may be lighter (wahu) for travel in the other realms. They will also paint their faces and adorn their bodies with seeds, feathers, and jaguar or wild pig canine necklaces. The Siona say that some of these adornments were received in previous rituals when the ally spirits from the other side threw them down to them. These adornments, along with sweet smelling herbs, are important in attracting the beautiful ally spirits, the Wahu people, who will help them in their journeys in the other side.

At sunset, those participating in the ceremony gather at the "Medicine House," bringing their hammocks to pass the night there. This small hut is located in the jungle away from the settlement and is used only for the purpose of hallucinogenic rituals.

At one end of the hut, the shaman sits upon a low bench with the ?uko prearation and its implements arranged on a small table in front of him. These include a chalice-like goblet made of clay with a small clay bowl stacked upon it, a bowl of a tree sap to one side of it, and a whisk of dried leaves on the other. The sap is classified as being "fresh" (wahu) and is drunk during the ceremony to create the sensation of freshness while intoxicated with the hallucinogen. The wisk is used during the ceremony to ritually prepare the ?uko before drinking it and also to cleanse participants and patients in the ceremony.

About seven or eight o'clock, the shaman begins to prepare the ?uko in the chalice in order to rid it of possible harmful effects. A larger pot of ?uko is placed on the floor next to him for use during the night. He sings and shakes the leaf whisk over the brew. Next he prays over it so that it inspires the visions desired. This is done by invoking in song the visions and spirits that the shaman wants to see. Each ritual is addressed to a specific supernatural realm or spirit the shaman wishes to see, and thus this preparation is a deliberate attempt to bring about the desired visions. After the invocation is complete, the shaman purs the first bowl and quickly drinks it, testing to see what kind of visions it will give. He may drink up to three bowls, each time performing the same ritual until the desired visions occur. If the affects desired are not achieved but instead prove to be unpleasant, the shaman destroys the ?uko and ends the ceremony, asserting that the drug has been damaged by a spirit. However, if the visions occur as expected, the shaman begins to sing of the sights that he is seeing on the "other side." This is the signal for his assistants to bring him his large feather crown and feather staff made of scarlet macaw feathers. It is said that the Sun spirit wears a similar crown in his journey across the sky each

each day and that a scarlet macaw sits upon his shoulder. Others present now request that they receive a bowl to drink. Each receives one after it has been ritually prepared. The group drinks from three to five times during the night, waiting an hour or two between each dose. After drinking, each person returns to his hammock to wait for the visions. During intoxication, they may be quite agitated or lie in silence. The shaman and his assistants sing and wildly stomp around the house. The shaman also growls, runs in and out of the hut, and occasionally climbs the rafters. Much of his singing is devoted to descriptions of the spirits, their clothing, their designs and colors. He also plays music from small reed pipes which are said to have come from the spirits during a previous ritual.

When the Siona describe this ritual, they concentrate on how all these antics are seen in the other side. The other side becomes a reality for them and the worlds of spirits and men blend. They say that everything is transformed into a brilliance and beauty unequalled in this reality. The shaman's sons are addressed to the spirits, and in the other side one hears the spirits reply and sees them descend. The special ally spirits, the Wahu People, are the first to come. They are adorned in clothing and ornaments similar to those of the Siona but far more beautiful and intricate in their design and colors. All the visions take on the colors that the shaman intends them to have. Music fills the air as the shaman and spirits play the special reed flutes. The shaman also evokes beautiful music from the bowl of sap, from the end of his feather staff, and from pieces of wild cane that grow along the Putumayo River and the Heaven River in the sky. Small nuts and other items from the Wahu People fall to them when the shaman climbs the rafters of the hut. The participants also see the shaman become an animal of the jungle as he "puts on the clothing" of the jaguar, wild pig, or anaconda. When he leaves the medicine house, they know he is travelling to the jaguar's house in the jungle, to the anaconda's house in the river, or to other spirits' houses. The participants may also travel with him, climbing on the back of a large anaconda who transports them to the other realms.

If the ritual is a curing ceremony, the shaman travels in the other side to find the offending spirit and bargain with him to save the patient. He must have sufficient dau inside of him to know the spirit's song and thus be able to speak with him. Otherwise he is helpless to counteract the spiritual cause of the illness. On this side, he ritually cleans the patient with the leaf whisk, chanting sacred songs. One patient told me how he saw the Wahu People descend to the whisk as the shaman sang. He also runs about, gesturing to the spirits, stomping and whistling, and plays a pan pipe. He sucks areas of the patient's body attempting to draw out the dau. Although not visible in this reality, The siona say that on the other side one can actually see the dau that he withdraws from the patient. He exams the dau to determine a prognosis of the case. If he finds it to be all black or rotten, he cannot save the patient. If it is clear, or wahu, in parts, there is hope for a cure. Dramatically he throws this substance away, sending it back to it origin.

Sometime before dawn, the activity begins to slow down as the people return to "this side." They drink a brew called "metal beverage," that has been specially prepared for ending the ceremony. The shaman then interprets the visions, drawing upon his knowledge of symbolic elements which he saw. In a curing session, he explains the supernatural cause and his success in ealing with the cause. Generally he will implicate some individual, generally a rival shaman, for instigating the supernatural attack. He instructs the patient in the specific kinds of nonhallucinogenic medicines that should be taken. After a hunting ritual, he tells of the results of his bargaining with the master spirit of the animals, explaining where and when game will be found. He also relates what he learned about the future or any other significant information.

The hallucinogenic ritual is a particularly powerful experience that blends the two realities. Like all rituals, it fuses the concrete and supernatural world through a set of symbolic forms which sum up the Siona's conception of cosmic order. Every object and act in the ritual is a representation of the other reality: the delicate face designs of the shaman are copies of those seen on the Wahu People; the furniture and pots are replicas of their furniture; the shaman's crown replicates that of the Sun spirit; the songs are the spirits songs; and so on. Moreover, the ritual is a drama of the forces and influences. conceptualized in the terms ?uko, wahu, dau, and hun?i. ?Uko activates the Siona's power to see into the other realm in order to understand the real reality behind events and to influence forces to help maintain a state of well-being. Participants in the ritual have fasted and purged themselves to be pure and wahu for the travels. During the night, the sap is drunk so they will continue to be wahu. The shaman's dau is the source of his headership in the rite and his ability to protect them from intruding malevolent spirits and fearful visions. A curing ceremony is a ritual battle of the forces of dau possessed by different individuals and spirits. The shaman uses his own dau to battle that evil dau in the patient that has been sent by a spirit or other shaman. The outcome of the battle will be health or death, depending upon the one in the battle who possesses the greatest amount of dau.

The ritual not only presents the conceptions of the cosmic order in a very realistic way, but also induces very strong moods and motivations associated with those conceptions, emotions of elation, hope, fear, and anxiety strong enough to color the activities of daily life. These moods permeate the ritual. There is a sense of elation over the prospect of travel with the shaman into the other side which is so magnificent and beautiful. There is hope of favorably influencing the spirits. In cases of illness, there is hope that those travels will lead to a cure for the patient. At the same time, the entire ritual is approached with anxiety and fear that all may not go well and that one will enter the realms of the evil spirits to become entangled with them. There is blackness instead of light, and frightening spirits with big ears and long tongues attempt to tie one up. One may never return to this side or return ill with a permanently damaged dau that might prohibit him from ever systematically taking the drug again. Thus, the rituals are not a light matter. The pre-ritual observances, rituals in their own right, work to allay this anxiety but at the same time to remind the individual of the dangers of the journey. The shaman himself is the embodiment of both these moods. This is clearly expressed in his transformation into the jaguar during the ritual. He presents power that can help restore forces in favor of those who ask his help, yet at the same time, he has the potential to use that power against those same people. Moreover, he can be damaged in the hallucinogenic travels. Through possession of dau he embodies power, yet he also may face a power greater than his, and this incorporates the anxiety held by all in the ceremony. The ritual dramatizes the double nature of ?uko and dau which create opposite feelings in the Siona. Both can be utilized for the benefit of one, but if these concrete representations are angered or damaged, the forces will turn against one. This double edged quality of the two is very real in the hallucinogenic experience, for indeed many novices and shamans have experienced bad visions and have fallen ill, later unable to drink the hallucinogen without recurrent bad visions. Many Siona who can no longer take the drug accuse the shaman administering the drug to them as the culprit damaging their visions. The fears and anxieties inherent in the experience are carried with the Siona from the ritual back into common sense reality, motivating them to live a life as if these fears were normal, given the way the world really is as depicted in the visions they have seen.

Geertz maintains that the power of ritual extends beyond the ritual itself, that the individual leaves changed, and in turn common sense reality is changed as the person places it in the context of the formulation of order experienced in the ritual. The Siona consciously recognize this change in the individual. All Siona men are expected to ingest a sufficient amount ?uko as youth so that they are able to leave their bodies to see the other realms. The successive ingestion of the drug leaves within them dau that represents their power to see. This dau continues to build with each ingestion, and most young men hope that it will not be damaged so that they may become master shamans. Thus, for the Siona, one literally leaves the ritual changed and must live his life according to taboos and mores that will protect the dau.[9] Although they do not possess dau, women must also obey mores intended to keep the dau from pollution, such as retiring to the menstrual hut during menses.

The way in which the two realities are blended in the ritual with particular emotional force can now be seen clearly. The key concepts of Siona world view represented in the terms described here take on concrete symbolic forms that induce strong emotions. In the case of the curing ritual, the participants witness an actual battle, as the shaman jaguar works his dau, removes dau from the patient, and sings and battles with the malevolent spirits. Moreover, these concrete representations have an existence outside the ritual. Immature plants and animals are wahu. Healthy people are wahu. Shamans and most adult men are "delicate" because of their dau; sick people have dau and are dying, and so forth. The dramatization of the general conceptions of order via concrete symbols in an emotionally charged and uniquely realistic ritual fuses together the imagined and common sense realities.

As the Siona carry out the routine of their daily lives, they are constantly aware of the two sides of reality. While a hunter walks through the jungle, he is continually aware of the other side of his reality and more concerned about the dangers coming from there than those coming from nature. He applied an ?uko in the morning to protect him and also one to his dog to make him a better hunter. He knows that the trees appear as spirit houses in the other side and that certain locations, such as small natural clearings in the virgin jungle, are the house sites of certain dangerous spirits. He must be ever aware that the beings in the other side could afflict him with illness and misfortune were he to break some taboo associated with them or suddenly mistake a spirit for a familiar person and actually follow him into the realm of the other side. Once there, nothing appears as it is in this side, and the hunter may wander from spirit house to spirit house, not knowing how to find his way home again. The spirits will offer him rotten chicha. If he drinks it, he will be lost forever. Many hunters have perished, lost forever in the jungle. A few lucky ones, aided by a shaman "travelling" in a hallucinogenic trance, have returned to tell of the other reality they saw.

In the same way, the Siona woman goes about her daily tasks, well aware of the hidden reality and the need to influence it favorably. She applies an ?uko to her digging stick in the garden to help the manioc grow large. When she washes clothes in the river or fetches water, she is aware of the dangerous hours at the river when the spirits are active. She also knows that it is dangerous to take her child out during certain hours of the day or pass too near certain trees known to contain dangerous spirits. Children are particularly susceptible to spirit attacks, and she often applies an ?uko to protect her baby. She will apply different kinds of ?uko to make the baby grow and to be strong and willing to perform proper tasks as an adult.

The quality of Siona interpersonal relations, too, is affected by the world view and moods expressed in the ritual. There is little overt conflict between the Siona as they seek to maintain peace with their relatives and neighbors. Yet any serious illness or misfortune stirs up rumors and accusations among the Siona as they try to interpret who has been angered enough to perform the sorcery causing the illness. The shaman has the ultimate authority to locate the actual offender, but a great amount of discussion surrounding any misfortune or illness centers on the possible motives that others might have for wishing harm. Any strange event or object that holds within it the symbolic qualities associated with dau will be analyzed and considered in great detail during daily conversations.

That which makes the Siona ritual particularly powerful does not lie so much in the ritual dramatization of the key conceptions of the cosmic order, as all rituals do this. It is the particular use of hallucinogenic visions as the major aid in transforming this reality and fusing it with the ultimate reality in a highly emotional and visual way. The hallucinogenic experience is a powerful one of the unconscious. What the Siona manage to do with their ritual is harness and channel this experience into culturally directed visions.[10] No hallucinogenic ceremony can be conducted without the presence of a shaman, the expert in travelling in the visionary realm. His role is to guide others through the realities that are visited during the night. He also must protect them from the dangers of such a journey. He sets the themes of the visions they will see. When he invokes the ?uko prior to drinking it, the participants are informed of where they will be travelling. To guide them once they are under the influence of the hallucinogen, his songs include details of what he is seeing. The spirits and their designs in his songs are not unknown to the Siona. The design motifs adorn the painted faces of the elders, the decorated pots, and other artifacts, including the clothing in times past. Much Siona oral literature includes descriptions of the spirits and journeys to see them. They are familiar with the other realms through myth, and the visionary experience gives them a particularly powerful knowledge and experience of the cosmic order. It seems reasonable to conclude, then, that the hallucinogenic aspect of the ritual gives it a singularly powerful ability to fuse the imagined and common sense realities. At the same time, it induces strong moods and motivations to adopt this vision of the world in common sense reality.

Summary:

   Siona cosmology and ritual are central to the entire culture. The cosmic order depicted in them pervades all aspects of everyday behavior, both in the Siona's observance of a large number of ritual practices and taboos and in their interpersonal relations. I have tried to show that perhaps one key to the pervasiveness of religion stems from the power of the hallucinogenic ritual to blend so successfully the imagined and commonsense world. I do not wish to say that there are not other means of accomplishing this. Geertz has already demonstrated that this is so in his description of ritual in Bali.[11] The Balinese use an emotional theatrical experience to induce a trance that allows them to cross the threshold into another order of existence. The Siona, however, use the visionary experience, equally powerful in the emotions and sense of reality it conveys. The hallucinogenic experience, as developed by the Siona into a cultural channeling of the visions, lends to the cosmological formulation of order a particularly strong authoritative experience which affirms that it is the "really real." The centrality of the ritual to Siona cosmology and life seems to be substantiated by the changes the Siona on the Putumayo are currently undergoing as they adapt to modern society. With the encroachment of whites in their former territory, few Siona youth have sought apprenticeships with master shamans. Of those that have, none have been successful, for they have all been plagued by bad visions. Most claim that living so close to white society has made it impossible to maintain the proper taboos that protect dau from damage. The last Siona master shaman of the Putumayo died in the 1950's, and now the Siona must seek shamans of other tribes or travel long distances to participate in the ritual. The elders evidence anxiety about living in a world whose workings they can no longer see and attempt to influence as in the past when the rituals were routinely held for the benefit of the community. While the youth hold the basic cultural suppositions about the world, few have participated intensively in the hallucinogenic rituals. They are increasingly drawn into the social and cultural spheres of the whites around them, abandoning many of the mores and taboos designed to protect dau. As the hallucinogenic ritual has passed among the Siona of the Putumayo, so will the Siona culture when the elders who participated in the ritual are gone. The Siona world view derives much of its authority from the renewal and reaffirmation given to it by the ritual. Without the authoritative experience of the ritual, the system as an ordered whole will not persist in the face of increasing contact with Western culture.

1. The data upon which this work is based were gathered during eighteen months of fieldwork in Colombia between 1970 and 1972. The study was supported in part by the Tulane University International Center for Medical Research grant AI-10050 from NIAID, NIH, U. S. Public Health Service.

2. Clifford Geertz, "Religion as a Cultural System," Anthropological Approaches to the Study of Religion (London, Tavistock Publications, 1966), pp. 1-46.

3. Ibid., p. 4.

4. Clifford Geertz, "Ethos, World View, and the Analysis of Sacred Symbols," The Interpretation of Cultures (New York, Basic Books, Inc., 1973), p. 127.

5. Ibid.

6. "Religion as a Cultural System," p. 38.

7. The u in uko and wahu is written phonetically as /i/, a high central vowel. Siona is a Western Tukanoan language. The Siona on the Putumayo are bilingual in Siona and Spanish. The major portion of the research was conducted in their own language.

8. "Religion as a Cultural System," p. 5.

9. Although women can participate in the rituals, very few women have become shamans. The Siona say that frequent ingestion of the hallucinogen causes sterility in women, and since their prime role is that of mother, women do not ingest the drug as often as men. No woman was ever said to possess dau as the substance gained from the drug.

10. See my article "Yage among the Siona: Cultural Patterns in Visions," Spirits, Shamans, and Stars: Perspectives from South America (Chicago, Aldine Publishing Co., projected date 1979), for a full explanation of culturally directed visions.

11. In "Religion as a Cultural System," p. 32, Geertz demonstrates that the Bali are also projected out to the common place world via a mass trance induced by the theatrical performance they are watching.

CHAPTER FIVE

"The Concept of 'Meaning' in Religion and Culture: A Dialogue

Between Anthropology and Theology"

John H. Morgan
University of Texas

THE CONCEPT OF "MEANING" IN RELIGION AND CULTURE:
Toward a Dialogue Between Theology and Anthropology*

" . . . events are not just there and happen, but they
have a meaning and happen because of that meaning."
— Max Weber

No one questions the truism which says that the concept of "meaning" is occupying a fundamental seat in contemporary thought. "The view of man as a symbolizing, conceptualizing, meaning-seeking animal . . . opens a whole new approach . . . to the analysis of religion," says Clifford Geertz of the Institute of Advanced Studies at Princeton.[1] And his philosophy mentor, Susan Langer, has observed that "the concept of meaning, in all its varieties, is the dominant philosophical concept of our time."[2] No stroke of brilliant insight is needed to notice that the concept of "meaning" has experienced ascendancy among the philosophers and theologians of our day far more than among the social scientists, at least in the cases where the former have spoken of man-as-experiential and the latter of man-as-behavioral. "No age," writes Heidegger in his KANT AND THE PROBLEM OF METAPHYSICS, "has known so much, and so many different things, about man as ours . . . And no age has known less than ours of what man is." The correlation between the ascendancy of the concept of "meaning" and the growing experience of bafflement about who and what man is can hardly be considered accidental. The

---

*The research for this paper was presented in modified form before the American Academy of Religion Annual Meeting in Washington, D. C., 1974, and before the American Anthropological Association Annual Meeting in Mexico City, 1974.

problem which is explicated by these two ingredients is man himself. "We are the first epoch," says Scheler, "in which man has become fully and thoroughly 'problematic' to himself; in which he no longer knows what he essentially is, but at the same time also knows that he does not know."[3]

The gaining of public consensus is not the issue, but rather the issue is the way in which the problem of meaning is to be articulated and addressed. Heidegger and Scheler would have meaning considered in terms of being, whereas Rabbi Heschel would reverse the order: "We have expressed the problem of man in the form of asking: What is being human? . . . Human being is never sheer being; it is always involved in meaning."[4] When considering the concept of "meaning" as a problem, we are in the realm of the uniquely human experience of reflective inquiry centered upon life-as-personal and not some abstract metaphysical category. "The dimension of meaning," continues Heschel, "is as indigenous to his being human as the dimension of space is to stars and stones . . . Human being is either coming into meaning or betraying it."[5]

There is no neutral ground in the experience of meaning. Meaning is experientially personal by definition, and its opposite is equally experientially existential, i.e., meaninglessness. Meaning/meaninglessness are not metaphysical categories but are categories of actual human encounter. Heschel again speaks to the relationship between being and meaning.

> Mental anguish is occasioned more by the experience or fear of meaningless being, of meaningless events, than by the mystery of being, by the absence

of being, or by the fear of non-being . . . The problem of being and the problem of meaning of being are coexitensive. In regard to man, the first problem refers to what he is in terms of his own existence, human being as it is; the second refers to what man means in terms larger than himself, being in terms of meaning.[6]

Some of the central questions raised through our wandering amid German phenomenology and Jewish philosophy must await our revisit later. For now, we must come back to Clifford Geertz's observations about man as a "meaning-seeking animal." Geertz is the latest and by far the most important anthropologist in several generations to employ this concept of meaning in any significant fashion, and he uses it in his definitions of religion and culture as we shall continue to point out. "Whatever else religion may be," Geertz says, "it is in part an attempt (of an implicit and directly felt rather than explicit and consciously thought-about sort) to conserve the fund of general meanings in terms of which each individual interprets his experience and organizes his conduct . . . "[7] Therefore, for a serious anthropological analysis of religion and culture to occur, Geertz is suggesting that the nature and function of "general meanings" must be analyzed. This is the first major attempt within anthropology to utilize the category of meaning as an integral part of the analysis of religion.[8]

Furthermore, in addition to religion, Geertz is suggesting that culture analysis must also cope with the category of meaning. "The culture concept to which I adhere . . . denotes an historically transmitted pattern of meanings embodied in symbols, a system of inherited conceptions expressed in symbolic forms by means of which men communicate, perpetuate, and develop their knowledge about and attitudes toward life."[9] The movement, demonstrated here, beyond definitions of the classical sort which defined culture as "learned human behavior" and "the way of life of a group of people"[10] to a conceptual framework which necessitates dealing in what Langer has called "our stock in trade," i.e., sign, symbol, denotation, signification, communication, suggests a shift in emphasis in culture analysis from the "doings" of man to "experiential meaningfulness of tradition (man-in-community)." What else does the term meaning as used by Geertz imply than this?

Meaning as human experience is that which constitutes the sine qua non of culture, and so likewise with religion. "Every religion," says the theological anthropologist Robley Edward Whitson, "has come into existence at a point of crisis in the meaning of a community, and remains in existence as long as it continues to make possible the positive confrontation of succeeding crises."[11] Meaning is not only the core of religion, but, says Whitson, it constitutes the essential experience of a community of people out of which religion is generated. This relationship between meaning-as-experience and religion is simultaneously communal and individual in expression: " . . . religious traditions are always necessarily concerned with the meaning of man not simply as an isolated individual but as a community as well."[12]

The same year that Geertz's article on "Religion as a Cultural System" appeared (1968), a collection of Paul Tillich's essays on his notion of a theology of culture appeared. The concept of meaning played a vital role in his treatment of the relationship between religion and culture, and in the following year, a collection of his essays entitled, WHAT IS RELIGION? appeared, with his most articulate and exhausive treatment of this idea. Tillich was primarily a philosopher of religion who understood his task to be to delineate a "philosophy of meaning (which could engage) in dialogue with any historical religion . . . (a consideration of man and his) relatedness to the Unconditional in terms of meaning."[13] Having been deeply influenced by the phenomenology of being of Heidegger and the existentialist thought of his day, Tillich combined a quest for a convergence of being-and-meaning in terms of a category called "meaning-reality," a term incorporating both the experience of meaning and its ground of Unconditionality.

"Meaning," explains Tillich, "is the common characteristic and the ultimate unity of the theoretical and the practical sphere of spirit, of scientific and aesthetic, of legal and social structures . . . Hence, the theory of the structure of meaning-reality, i.e., philosophy, is the theory of the principles of meaning, and its first task is an analysis of meaning itself . . . "[14] As Tillich begins to develop a theory of meaning, he is driven by a complementing relationship between an ontology of being and an anthropology of meaning — a concern for religion and culture which centers upon the ground of meaning-reality. Yet, Tillich is not unaware of the grave and difficult problems awaiting him.[15] Tillich has called the pursuit of "the meaning of meaning a paradoxical enterprise . . . " In spite of these recognized problems, Tillich has suggested three elements in any analysis of meaning — in religion and culture — which must be considered. First, the interconnectedness of meaning within all separate meanings must center or face meaninglessness. Second, the recognition of the ultimate meaning of all meaning and thus of every particular meaning. And third, the recognition of the imperative upon every particular meaning to fulfill the unconditioned meaning. There is no meaning which stands alone — meanings are connected into a total meaning-system which legitimize each separate meaning as they totally reside in the Unconditioned Meaning. "Even the totality of meaning," concludes Tillich, "need not be meaningful, but rather could disappear, like every particular meaning, in the abyss of meaninglessness, if the presupposition of an unconditioned meaningfulness were not alive in every act of meaning."[16] For Tillich, to raise the question or possibility of meaninglessness is to have already posited meaning — Buber's critique of Nietzsche and Sartre is precisely here, viz., how can one raise the question of meaningless existence without having by that very question established a prior condition of meaning. Heschel shall speak poignantly to this point later.

EXPRESSIONS OF MEANING

CULTURE AS MEANING

Under the philosophical influence of Susan Langer, Geertz has brought the term "meaning" fully into anthropological parlance. Those of us who have taken to its usage have, consequently and for good or ill, sought to establish our own identity (almost) with the characterization of our work as "symbolic anthropology." Though I must here decline to define such an exotically sounding methodology, it does, however, seem reasonable to expect that our task as anthropologists is somehow to come to terms with a definition of culture (the <u>sine qua non</u> of our disciplinary subject-matter) as "an historically transmitted pattern of meanings embodied in symbols . . ."[17] Geertz is not a radical behaviorist who readily correlates the skinnerian box activity of mice to human social interaction. Nor is he a mushy humanist who quickly moves from a token deference to data to a posture as moralist.

Seriously and persistently, Geertz attempts to do his work as analyzer of cultural meanings in the context of the actually lived experience of men in human community — paying attention to the bio-behavioral while simultaneously maintaining sensitivity to the actual patterns of meanings socially transmitted through culture. In recognizing with Langer that "the concept of meaning . . . is the dominant philosophical concept of our time," he attempts to demonstrate the relevance of the concept in an analysis of culture.

Though demonstrating a positive sensitivity to the indispensable role of philosophy in theoretical anthropology,[18] Geertz does not attempt to defend the term "meaning" philosophically, but rather leaves that to Langer. "The analysis of 'meaning'," suggests Langer, "has had a peculiarly difficult history . . . a good deal of controversy has been wasted on the subject of the correct way, the meaning of 'meaning'."[19] However unfortunate the time wasted might be among philosophers, anthropologists have not dwelt upon the concept and, as Geertz demonstrates, are grateful for a theory of meaning conducive to the analysis of culture.

Though Langer decries the wasted time, she herself propounds what hopefully is an elastic and functional characterization if not a definition: "There is in fact no quality of meaning, its essence lies in the realm of logic, where one does not deal with qualities, but only with relations . . . 'Meaning is not a quality, but a function of a term.' A function is a pattern viewed with reference to one specific term round which it centers . . . "[20] Three points emerge in this passage from Langer, the third of which must demand our attention, necessarily leaving the first two unattended. First, from the point of view of an ontological philosophy of religion as developed by Tillich and Heschel which speaks to the relationship of being to meaning, the shallowness of Langer's functional versus ontological characterization is a bit disappointing. Second, Langer has characterized meaning as a function and function as a pattern, and in this sequential definition wherein Geertz finds his word "pattern," there is possible grounds for suggesting that Geertz's definition of culture is crypto-functionalistic by design if not by intention.

These two questions must await another essay. For now, attention must be focused upon the third point, viz., the utilization by Geertz of Langer's development of the term meaning. Langer continues her inquiry into the logic and function of meaning, and concludes that there "are three . . . familiar meanings of the word, 'meaning,' signification, denotation, and connotation."[21] These three familiar meanings — epitomized in the function of cultural symbols — become important ingredients in Geertz's use of meaning and his understanding of the nature of symbol. " . . . (C)ulture patterns," observes Geertz, "have an intrinsic double aspect:

they give meaning, i.e., objective conceptual form, to social and psychological reality both by shaping themselves to it and by shaping it to themselves . . . It is, in fact, this double aspect which sets true symbols off from other sorts of significative forms."[22] Geertz is consistent with Langer in attributing to symbols as meaning-bearers an "objective conceptual form," Langer having stressed repeatedly the conceptual nature of symbol as meaning. For example, Langer has proposed "a definition of 'symbol' based on this formulative function, by means of which some sort of conception is always abstracted from any symbolized experience."[23] As carried out in culture analysis by Geertz, Langer first called for a study of meaning and symbol which involved logical processes of conceptualization — a philosophical foundation upon which an anthropology of culture-meaning could easily find stability. In another place, Langer brought together all three terms — symbol, meaning, conceptualizing — in one succinct statement: "Wherever a symbol operates, there is meaning; and conversely . . . No symbol is exempt from the office of logical formulation, of conceptualizing what it conveys: however simple its import, or however great, this import is a meaning, and therefore an element for understanding."[24]

Having been substantially informed by Langer's "new key" philosophy, Geertz goes back to his own efforts at culture analysis with a solid philosophical foundation.[25] Possessed with a passion to come to terms with meaning as a fundamental ingredient in human culture, Geertz sets out to articulate the distinction between culture and social system — the confusion of the two having been a continual plague for social scientific theorizing especially in the analysis of social and cultural change — by noting that culture is "an ordered system of meaning and of symbol, in terms of which social interaction takes place . . . " whereas a social system is "a pattern of social interaction itself . . . "[26] This distinction gave Geertz more precision in his utilization of the variables within each of the two categories of culture and social system, and also led to a deeper understanding of the coextensive elements between them — what Geertz later came to call the "socio-cultural." In view of this elucidated distinction, Geertz proceeded to characterize "culture (as) the fabric of meaning in terms of which human beings interpret their experience and guide their action" whereas "social structure is the form that action takes, the actually existing network of social relations."[27] If Geertz is, indeed, a functionalist, as our innuendo ventured to suggest earlier, he is a revisionist-functionalist, for he seeks to come to grips with dimensions of human culture, particularly meaning, which have heretofore gone unattended by traditional functionalism.[28]

In spite of the broadened and deepened scope of the concept of meaning developed by Langer and employed by Geertz, the absence in their usage of the ontological and existential dimensions of meaning leave their treatment of culture as an expression of meaning incomplete. The incompleteness is accentuated by means of a simple juxtaposition of definitions of Heschel's philosophical task and that of Langer's. The latter has defined philosophy as "the systematic study of meanings . . . " and culture as "the symbolic expression of developed habitual ways of feeling."[29] As far as they go, there is no quarrel with these definitions. However, there is something lacking in the depth of understanding suggested by such an ambiguously shallow notion as "habitual ways of feeling." Heschel defines philosophy as that which "man dares to do with his ultimate surmise of the meaning of existence . . . "[30] Though "habitual ways of feeling" seems a bit mechanistic and timid, Heschel's employment of "ultimate surmise of the meaning of existence" does not. The here-and-now experiential encounter with meaning implies more than just feeling — it speaks of the profoundly existential. Heschel continues: "Imbedded in the mind is a certainty that the state of existence and the state of meaning stand in a relation to each other, that life is assessable in terms of meaning."[31]

The truly human experience of being is not just an involvement in a functional pattern of habitually established feelings, but rather being human qua human being is constituted by means of a synthesis of existence and meaning. "The will to meaning and the certainty of the legitimacy of our striving to ascertain it," concludes Heschel, "are as intrinsically human as the will to live and the certainty of being alive."[32] Beyond the socio-cultural function of meaning-systems lies the uniquely human grasp for the Essential below/above the existential; but the encounter with the fundamentally essential quality of meaning does not lie within the existential itself — otherwise man's experience of meaning is built upon a tautology which says that existential meaning is intrinsically self-validating. Human being cannot establish his own meaning by means of his being human. "What we are in search of," says Heschel, "is not meaning for me, an idea to satisfy my conscience, but rather a meaning transcending me, ultimate relevance of human being."[33] Only by so doing can man hope to find that beyond himself which affirms meaning in himself. Heschel contends, differing somewhat from Tillich's Heideggerian emphasis on the primacy of being, that being for man can have meaning only in terms of man's "meaning in being." "The quest of the meaning of being," argues Heschel, "is a quest for that which surpasses being, expressing insufficiency of sheer being. Meaning and being are . . . not coextensive. Meaning is a primary category not reducible to being as such . . . Existence is not acceptance of being, but relating it to meaning; and his unique problem is not how to come into being, but how to come into meaning."[34]

The philosophies of Tillich and Heschel have added another dimension to our consideration of culture as an expression of meaning, and though the implications are somewhat differently drawn from Geertz and Langer as over against Heschel and Tillich, these implications do not appear to be inexorably antipathetic. The moods are different and must be held in creative tension, as indicated in our closing quotes to this part of the essay:

> Culture, creating a universe of meaning, does not create this universe in the empty space of mere validity. It creates meaning as the actualization of what is potential in the bearer of the spirit — in man . . .35

> The concept of culture I espouse . . . is essentially a semiotic one. Believing, with Max Weber, that man is an animal suspended in webs of significance he himself has spun, I take culture to be those webs, and the analysis of it to be therefore not an experiential science in search of law but an interpretive one in search of meaning . . . Meaning, that elusive and ill-defined pseudoentity we were once more than content to leave philosophers and literary critics to fumble with, has now come back into the heart of our discipline.36

RELIGION AS MEANING

Having considered the strength and weaknesses of Geertz's definition of culture as "historically transmitted pattern of meanings embodied in a complex of symbols," we come now to an equally difficult task (alluded to in the introductory comments wherein meaning and religion were readily linked as mutually relatable categories of human experience) of analyzing religion as an expression of meaning. Without doubt, no category of human experience has been the topic of so much controversy, so much polemic, so much research, as that of religion. And though we do not pretend a resolution of the issues of controversy, we do intend to investigate the various ways in which religion has been considered an expression of meaning and/or meaninglessness. In addition to consulting Geertz and Tillich on this questions, we have drawn extensively from the works of Peter Berger, a sociologist of religion, and Robley Edward Whitson, a theological anthropologist.[37]

Of the most lucid contemporary social scientists who have addressed the problems and issues in the study of religion, none have been more insightfully stimulating and challenging than Peter Berger. While demonstrating in the intellectual genre of Geertz, a scientific methodology of unquestionable integrity, Berger has continued to demonstrate a humanistic sensitivity to the multi-dimensionality of religious phenomena. He is rigorous in the restrictions he places upon his own judgments and conclusions drawn from his scientific analysis of the social dimension of religion. With Bellah, he is critical of a positivistic social science which too easily reduces the complexities of religious phenomena to easily-handled reductionistic behaviorisms.

Berger has suggested, in the context of an analysis of the history of ideas called sociology of knowledge,[38] that this positivistic-reductionistic trend has taken on increasing prominance since Feuerbach. "A good case could be made,"

Berger points out, "that not only Marx's and Freud's treatment of religion, but the entire historical-psychological-sociological analysis of religious phenomena since Feuerbach has been primarily a vast elaboration (of the position that religion) instead of (being) a dialogue between man and superhuman reality, religion became a sort of human monologue."[39] In our consideration of religion as meaning, Berger confronts us here with a two-fold danger — on the one hand, of reducing the experience of meaning to simply functional analysis as is the impending danger for Geertz nurtured by Langer, and on the other hand, of instigating a "human monologue" (Berger) in terms of which meaning is defined exclusively in existential terms with no reference or room for the Essential, or the "transcendent" as Heschel chose to call it, or the "Unconditioned" as in Tillich.

Meaning is a category of human experience, but it is not summarily defined by that observation. "The implication of the rootage of religion in human activity is not that religion is always a dependent variable in the history of a society, but rather that it derives its objective and subjective reality from human beings, who produce and reproduce it in their ongoing lives."[40] Religion as a complex of phenomena is subject to systematic analysis, for its objective manifestations eminate from actual people. No pretention is made here to study the "essence" of the religious phenomena, only their manifestations.[41]

Meaning, a category of human experience, is expressed existentially in human community and these expressions — cultural and religious — are observable and, thus, subject to analysis. That is not to say that meaning is "nothing but" its existential concretizations. Such a claim comes from positivism, and Berger and Geertz are radically opposed to a reductionism which precludes de facto the dimension of the Essential, the Transcendent, or the Unconditioned.[42] "The essential perspective of the sociological theory here proposed is that religion is to be understood as a human projection, grounded in specific infra-structures of human history."[43] Otherwise, how can an explanation be given for the integrality of cultural and religious expressions of meaning? The fallacy of Freud, Feuerbach, Marx, and all positivists and functionalists, says Berger, is the disastrous failure to discern that the human experience which gives rise to projection is not derived from the projection itself (a circularity of deception too transparent to be credible), but rather is prior to such projection. To the extent that religious behavior is "nothing but" this kind of self-deceptive circularity, Freud and Marx are justified in their attacks upon religion. But the quest for meaning as we are considering it here in the context of religion and culture is certainly beyond such attacks. The ascendancy of the category of meaning as a legitimate topic for discussion among anthropolpologists would appear to be proof enough of the accuracy of such an observation.

Walking that thin line between positivism and functionalism on the one hand and that of the human monologue-theory on the other, Geertz has put forth what is increasingly being considered the most useful definition of religion to date in the social sciences. Attempting to demonstrate the perimeters within which and the methodology by which the social sciences, especially anthropology, can legitimately analyze religious phenomena while simultaneously holding back any inclination to question the credibility of theology and phenomenology in their pursuit of the essence of religious experience, Geertz has put forth the following definition:

"Religion is 1) a system of symbols which acts to 2) establish powerful, persuasive, and long-lasting moods and motivations in men by 3) formulating conceptions of a general order of existence and 4) clothing these conceptions with such an aura of factuality that 5) the moods and motivations seem uniquely realistic."[44] The design, obviously, is not to construct a definitive definition which can exhaust all the dimensions of religious phenomena — how absurd such a notion would be! — but rather to construct a definition with intentional limitation and specificity of scope. Later, we will pursue a definition which more precisely centers upon meaning in an attempt to bring about a more analogous description of religion with that of culture which might better facilitate dialogue.

Concurring with but not limiting himself to Yinger who has defined religion as a "system of beliefs and practices by means of which a group of people struggles with . . . ultimate problems of human life,"[45] Geertz suggests that a fundamental characteristic (might we say "function"?) of religion is the address to the "problem of meaning" — meaning suggesting either purpose and direction to life or meaninglessness, chaos, pointless existence. "There are at least three points," says Geertz, "where chaos — a tumult of events which lack not just interpretation but interpretability — threatens to break in upon man at the limits of his analytic capacities, at the limits of his powers of endurance, and at the limits of his moral insight. Bafflement, suffering, and a sense of intractable ethical paradox are all . . . radical challenges . . . with which any religion, however 'primitive,' which hopes to persist must attempt somehow to cope."[46] Without doing violence to the social scientific perspective of Geertz, we can say that religion functions as an experientially motivated address to the problem of impending chaos in man's existential life.

Further, and under guidance from Tillich and Heschel, we can say that beyond, behind, or under this function to cope with bafflement, suffering, and inextricable ethical paradox lies the Essential Meaning of which these expressions in quest of existential meaning are enduring witnesses. This extension must, of course, be pursued in depth later in this study.

Geertz is not oblivious to this possible extension and logical elaboration of his position, nor is he antipathetic to such an endeavor. "The Problem of Meaning in each of its intergrading aspects . . . " continues Geertz, "is a matter of affirming, or at least recognizing, the inescapability of ignorance, pain, and injustice on the human plane while simultaneously denying that these irrationalities are characteristic of the world as a whole."[47] Even an elementary acquaintance with the history of the scientific study of culture and religion is sufficient to establish the qualitative if not special advance of Geertz's treatment of religion and culture from the point of view of meaning over efforts of the past (admirable if for no other reason than that they serve as preliminaries to the present effort). Within his definitional construct Geertz stands head and shoulders above all past efforts to understand religion and culture by the positivists and functionalists – the way is truly open for an honest dialogue between the social scientist, philosopher, and theologian. "The existence," Geertz concludes, "of bafflement, pain and moral paradox – of the Problem of Meaning – is one of the things that drive men toward belief in gods, devils, spirits, totemic principles, or the spiritual efficacy of cannibalism . . . but it is not the basis upon which those beliefs rests, but rather their most important field of application."[48] These expressions characteristic of religion are conveyed through cultural symbols all of which bespeak the problem of meaning — an existential meaning — for man against chaos and in pursuit of order.

Geertz lays no claim of competency in speaking to the "basis upon which belief rests," having intentionally focused his attention upon the problem of meaning as it is expressed in and through the cultural symbol-systems of man. If we can agree that Geertz has set the stage from an anthropological perspective for a dialogue with philosophy and theology, then we might agree that Robley E. Whitson has written the prologue if not the first scene of that play. Robley Whitson is an anthropologist by training, having been tutored at Fordham University under Professor J. Franklin Ewing. He is also a Roman Catholic priest by vocation, and a theologian by profession. The happy combination of anthropologist cum theologian has produced a most stimulating treatment of the COMING CONVERGENCE OF WORLD RE-LIGIONS (1971) — an ethnological approach to and perspective upon theological method. Among others, William Cenkner of the Catholic University has considered Whitson's study an unquestionable breakthrough in the analysis of the convergence of religions and a landmark in the dialogue between theological and ethnological method.[49]

In truly responsible anthropological form, Whitson begins with experiencing-man in his real social milieu. In seeking to define the theological method in terms of cultural context — the anthropological task in any dialogue with theology — Whitson states his point of beginning: "The formulation we seek must arise from within actual religious experience . . . to be authentic it must recognize and prize the very different heritages, for we can now see that each (religious tradition) at its core is unique . . . Some how the differing traditions . . . are to become dimensions of one another . . . "[50] Geertz, Berger, and Whitson in consort (more coincidentally than intentionally we suppose) with the liberal theological tradition following Schleiermacher begin with actual experience — a mutually agreeable starting point for social science and liberal theology. Later, in the context of a discussion of Berger's work, we will briefly consider the distinguishing characteristics of a liberal theology sensitive to both experience and cultural expression.

Whitson is concerned with the relationship between actual cultures and actual religions in terms of which a true convergence — not a syncretism — is occurring. The convergence is occurring at the point of actual experience, and thus religion and culture must be understood in an experiential context. "Religion as a process of asking-and-answering," begins Whitson, "is not an abstraction floating somewhere in space, but a human process; real people do the asking and answering from within the actual situation of their moments of living."[51] Denying the legitimacy of the functionalistic approach in the study of religion, Whitson plays upon the categories of actual experience and process — from within actual experience, man-in-community engages in the quest for life's meaning, i.e., the process of asking-and-answering. "Every religion," suggests Whitson, "has come into existence at a point of crisis in the meaning of a community, and remains in existence as long as it continues to make possible the positive confrontation of succeeding crises."[52] The concrete milieu of an actual community is that within which religion is generated. Religion comes at a time of "crisis in meaning" and vanishes when religion no longer speaks of meaning in an experientially validating manner. This crisis in meaning is not solely individual (as too much post-Nietzschean existentialism would deceive us into thinking),[53] but is within the human context of community. "Religious traditions are always necessarily concerned with the meaning of man," says Whitson, "not simply as an isolated individual but as a community as well."[54] Later, we will dwell more intensely upon Whitson's ethnological approach to theological method in our consideration of theology defined as the systematic analysis of religion.

The task Whitson has set for himself, what he has called "anthropologizing theology," constitutes the most important effort in this generation to establish a context for creative dialogue between anthropology and theology as they converge upon the experiential dynamic operative in religious and cultural contact and interaction. Whitson's convergence model brings together for the first time an analytic study of culture as meaning, exemplified brilliantly by Geertz, and an analytic study of religion as meaning, particularly provocatively done by Tillich. Tillich, being a philosopher of religion and self-labeled "theologian of culture," has not restricted his observational analysis as Geertz has done to the cultural manifestations, but feels a professional imperative not only to speak of religion and culture as meaning-systems, but to plumb for their gound of being, what he calls their "meaning-reality."

J. Luther Adams, a theologian of note and commentator on Tillich, has observed that, for Tillich, man "strives to fulfill the possibilities of being," being characterized as a "meaning-reality that is inescapable and which is never subject to manipulation with impunity . . ."[55] The heideggarian influence in the form of a phenomenology of being is obvious in Tillich's system. But he is not bound by this influence, but develops it to serve the theological task in addressing being as "meaning-reality," the "unconditionality of meaning" which is present in every act of the human spirit — theoretical, aesthetic, practical.[56] "Meaning," continues Adams in his preface to a collection of Tillich's essays, "is three-fold" for Tillich. "It is an awareness of a universal interconnection of meaning, an awareness of the ultimate meaningfulness of the interconnection of meaning, and an awareness of a demand to fulfill, to be obedient to, the ultimate, unconditional meaning-reality."[57] Though not inevitably anti-pathetic to Geertz, Tillich has necessarily gone beyond the realms of anthropological analysis of religion and culture as meaning-systems. In order to take account of that out of which existential meaning derives, the nature of meaning must be sough in terms larger than man to avoid the tautological problem mentioned earlier, and to avoid the existentialist trap of a human monologue, propounded by Nietzsche and Sartre, analyzed by Berger, and attacked by Heschel and Buber.

Meaning-reality, to use Tillich's term for the existential/essential duality of meaning as being, cannot be expressed in the raw, but rather must be experientially expressed through religio-cultural media, i.e., symbol-systems.[58] "Meaning finds expression in forms that have a particular content," explains Adams, "but form and content as such do not require more than relatedness to the interconnection of meaning . . . The more fundamental element . . . Tillich calls the Import of meaning (reminiscent of Hegel's Lectures on Aesthetics)."[59] Tillich, as we noted earlier, is profoundly sensitive to the cultural milieu within which all human experience occurs for existential meaning is transmitted through the forms and contents of culture.[60] The form and content of culture characterize the manner in which meaning

is portrayed, expressed, established, but form and content are only indirectly fo-

cused upon or responsible to the Unconditional which constitutes the source of all

existential meaning. That quality of meaning which distinguishes between culture

and religion Tillich has called "import."[61] "Authentic religion," then, can be de-

scribed as "directedness toward this import, directedness toward the Uncondi-

tional."[62]

With such a distinction between religion and culture based on the dimensions

of the experience of meaning, we have set before us an analytic structure which

allows of both the cultural and the theological. Culture is the expression of mean-

ing through its forms and contents indirectly addressed to Essential Meaning, the

Unconditional, whereas religion is the expression of meaning, imbedded in cultural

forms and contents, intentionally focused upon the Essential, the Unconditional,

as this ground, or meaning-reality is conveyed through its import of meaning.

Culture-meaning is singularly directed through its forms and contents; religion on

the other hand is double-directed because of its awareness of not only form and

content but also of import, i.e., towards "the conditioned forms of meaning and

their interreleations," and also towards "the unconditional meaning-reality which

is the ground of the import."

For Tillich, religion or culture cannot be spoken of in the absence of the

other, for they both convey meaning, granted the difference in direction and level

of intensity. "Culture is defined," therefore, "as lacking this double-directedness

(toward form and import): it is oriented only to the conditioned forms and the interreleation of meaning. Yet culture is substantially, if not intentionally, religious, for every meaning is supported by the unconditioned meaning-reality."[63] This notion that culture is substantially religious due to the necessary reliance of its existential meaning upon the unconditioned meaning-reality, is central to Tillich's thought, and from the point of view of an anthropological analysis of culture as meaning, offers a most positive possibility for dialogue.

Geertz and Tillich have made use of the concept of meaning in a manner heretofore ignored or overlooked, and though Geertz has contributed substantially to this growing climate of dialogue, Tillich has taken the first bold step. "In abbreviation," says Tillich in another place, "religion is the substance of culture, culture is the form of religion."[64] Whereas religion is intentionally focused upon the Unconditional by means of the import of meaning, culture is substantially focused upon the forms and contents of meaning and thus is religious by substance but not by design. For Tillich, the direction that expressions of meaning take becomes the distinguishing determinant between religion and culture, succinctly recorded in this quote from Tillich: "If consciousness is directed toward the particular forms of meaning and their unity, we have to do with culture, if it is directed toward the unconditioned meaning, toward the import of meaning, we have religion. Religion is directedness toward the Unconditional, and Culture is directedness toward the conditioned forms and their unity."[65]

Obviously, Tillich has begun with a task in mind which oversteps the aspirations as well as methodology of anthropology. And yet, I am not ready to dismiss this effort as simply ideology. If Tillich has defined culture in terms agreeable to good anthropology (of the kind demonstrated by Geertz) and if his definition of religion, though not substantially in anthropological terminology, is not antipathetic to anthropological method, then there is a beginning point for dialogue. We have been suggesting here that that dialogic point is the concept of meaning. Of course, in a pursuit of the dimensions of meaning in terms of religion and culture, we must finally come to some understanding as to the nature of the disciplines employed in our particular pursuit, i.e., anthropology and theology. By way of transition from religion and culture to theology and thropology, let us take one more look at Tillich's religion-culture relationship model:

> In the cultural act, therefore, the religious is substantial; in the religious act the cultural is formal. Culture is the sum total of all spiritual acts directed toward the fulfillment of particular forms of meaning and their unity. Religion is the sum total of all spiritual acts directed toward grasping the unconditioned import of meaning through the fulfillment of the unity of meaning . . . The field in which culture and religion meet is the common directedness toward the unity of meaning . . . In the sphere of knowledge culture is directedness toward the conditioned forms of existence and their unity. Religion in the sphere of knowledge is directedness toward the unconditionally existing as the ground and abyss of all particular claims and their unity.[66]

In terms of the dynamics of meaning operative in culture, as in religion, there is an "actualization" process at work which goes beyond a "creation" suggested by Sartre: "Culture, creating a universe of meaning," explains Tillich, "does not create this universe in the empty space of mere validity. It creates meaning as the actualization of what is potential in the bearer . . ."[67]

SYSTEMATICS OF MEANING

Culture and religion are expressions of meaning, the former through existential form and content, the latter through essential import. Therefore, a convergence of cultural and religious expression occurs with the concept of meaning – a multi-dimensional experience communicated through symbols.[68] Whereas culture and religion are convergent expressions of meaning, anthropology and theology must be understood to be disciplines addressed to the systematics of meaning, and as foot-noted above, the analysis of meaning will inevitably involve an analysis of the symbol as meaning-bearer.[69]

Religion as studied by anthropology involves a two-step operation, according to Geertz: "First, an analysis of the system of meanings embodied in the symbols which make up the religion proper, and second, the relating of these systems to social-structural and psychological processes."[70] Earlier we considered Geertz's treatment of the social and cultural as mutually related and neither intrinsically dominant. Geertz has attempted to demonstrate receptiveness to the various disciplinary approaches to religious studies, even phenomenology as the study of "religion proper," by way of suggesting a model of multi-disciplinary complementarity.

Anthropology is an interpretive science engaged in the search for meaning through a systematic analysis of culture – i.e., man's meaning embodied in symbols.[71] This precision of directedness upon culture implies a scientific method of categorizing. "Analysis," says Geertz, "is sorting out the structures of significance . . . and determining their ground and import."[72] If culture is the expression of meaning, and anthropology is the analysis of culture, then we can say that the fundamental task of anthropology put succinctly is the systematics of meaning – meaning here being the existential meaning of form and content. And this systematic analysis, of systematization of meaning necessitates an analysis of the psycho-socio-cultural structures/processes which constitute the framework of meaning.

An essential quality of the anthropological enterprise is its desire for universal application, for the cross-cultural perspective is the sine qua non of anthropological method. The benefit hoped for is the facilitation of what Geertz has called "the enlargement of the universe of human discourse." This sensitivity to the vast panorama of human experience in actual culture-systems plays a vital role in establishing credibility of interpretation as we approach diverse culture-systems of meaning. The analysis of juxtaposed culture patterns is an attempt to observe and understand "the degree to which its (any particular culture form) meaning varies according to the pattern of life by which it is informed . . ."[73] We are confronted with three alternative responses to this anthropological approach to culture and religion: 1) to be impressed with the dynamics of cultural diversity vigorously pursuing the analysis of various forms and contents, forgoing any philosophical speculation as to the implications of such an impression, 2) to be so impressed with cultural diversity that one concludes that life has no "ground" and the only absolute in reality is "relativity," or 3) to be informed by cultural diversity as form-and-content expressions of meaning which are understood to be reflections of meaning-reality. The discipline of anthropology, when strictly adhering to its definition as a science for the systematic analysis of socio-cultural phenomena, is bound to the first option — observation, description, understanding, and interpretation. Nowhere is the discipline forced to adhere either to the second or third options and when it does, it is either stepping into the circle of positivism (in the second option) or theology/philosophy (in the third option).

We can discount the second option from the start as antipathetic to the integrity of anthropology as a social science. (The second option, where tenaciously held to, has resulted in anthropology being reduced to an "ideological sect.") From the beginning of this inquiry, we have hoped to establish the possibility of an anthropology defined in terms of the first option engaging in a dialogue with theology, thus leading to a convergence of methods suggested in the third option — a method of religious-cultural analysis labelled by Tillich, theology of culture. But before we explore such a suggestion, let us hear Geertz once more on the vocation of anthropology:

> To look at the symbolic dimensions of social action — art, religion, ideology, science, law, morality, common sense — is not to turn away from the existential dilemmas of life for some empyrean realm of de-emotionalized forms; it is to plunge into the midst of them. The essential vocation of interpretive anthropology is not to answer our deepest questions, but to make available to us answers that others, guarding other sheep in other valleys, have given, and thus to include them in the consultable record of what man has said.[74]

We need not attempt a resolution here of the age-old philosophical dispute over whether the presence of order is in the world and thus discoverable or whether in the mind and thus constructable. The answer to such a problem, though desirable, is not a prerequisite ot our observation about man being driven to find/create order-system-category. This drive is suggestive of an imperative in human experience — no society exists without a conception of order in the world, of system in experience.[75] "The drive to make sense out of experience," says Geertz, "to give it form and order, is evidently as real and as pressing as the more familiar biological needs." This making "sense out of experience" is what we are calling the "systetematics of meaning." Though Geertz and Berger, as in the latter's statement, "Men are congenitally compelled to impose a meaningful order upon reality,"[76] seem to have resolved for themselves the issue of finding-or-creating order, we need not pass judgment upon that personal preference to concur with this apparent imperative of ordering or systematizing.

Though religion and culture are complementing expressions of meaning, the former through import, and the latter through form and content, there is more to meaning than just its experientially-based expression. Men seek to organize their expressions of meaning — no society is devoid of these systematizers.[77] And, as we have seen in Geertz's explanation of anthropology as an "interpretive science" which gave rise to our characterization of anthropology as the systematic analysis of culture-as-meaning, we can also suggest that in an attempt to understand religion-as-meaning, the human propensity for order has given rise to an intellectual enterprise engaged in the systematic analysis of religion-as-meaning, viz., theology. The social scientific approach to the study of religion, as demonstrated in Geertz, is a systematic analysis of the content and form of religious and cultural phenomena, whereas the theological approach to the study of religion, as demonstrated in Tillich, is a systematic analysis of the import of religious and cultural phenomena. Whereas Geertz says anthropology does not seek to understand the "basis of belief" but rather belief's manifestations, Tillich says that theology is an address to the basis of belief by means of belief's religious and cultural manifestations. To use the term theology in this manner calls for a substantive explanation if not defense, since the term, as with anthrpology,[78] has been defined in countless and often conflicting ways.[79]

The category of human experience which finds expressions through culture and religion, i.e., the experience of meaning, has occupied our time throughout this deliberation. That we have defined religion and culture in terms of experience must necessarily inform our definition of theology as it has our definition of anthropology. More precisely, we would have our theological method find itself converging with our anthropological method at the point of experiential meaning, and such a beginning point necessarily aligns our method with Schleiermacher and the liberal tradition in theology vis a vis Barth and the Neo-Orthodox tradition.[80]

Though Geertz (anthropology) and Bellah (sociology) have demonstrated, implicitly and unintentionally rather than explicitly and intentionally, a methodological openness to theological approaches to religion, Whitson (anthropology) and Berger (sociology) are without question the most important contemporary figures to attempt a formulation of the dialogue between the social sciences and theology.[81] Berger is seeking an "emancipation from this sequence of 'mood theologies'," so evident today in the market-place of theologians, e.g., the death-of-god theology of Altizer and company, the "somatic" theology of Norman O. Brown's Dionysian Christianity, the "ethnic theologies" of the Cone variety. Berger suggests that contemporary "theological thought revert to an anthropological starting point . . . " which necessitates an "anchorage in fundamental human experience . . . " whereby theological method could "seek out" the "signals of transcendence within the empirically given human situation."[82]

Berger is not seeking a "theological Esperanto," but is contending for a theological method (within any tradition of religious experience) which sees itself centered upon the actual "experience of the human situation." Theology as the systematics of religion must begin with religion, i.e., the experience of Essential Meaning embodied in a complex of symbols. Theology is the analysis of experience and its concomitant expressions, and is not fundamentally an elaboration of creeds or articles of faith, for these expressions, to the extent that they carry meaning are derivatives of experience. A theology addressed to the creeds is a theology once removed from the import of religion.

Berger has spoken to this conflict between experience and doctrine in terms of the categories of inductive faith — induction begins with experience, and deductive faith — deduction begins with idea. "Put simply," explains Berger, "indictive faith moves from human experience to statements about God, deductive faith from statements about God to interpretations of human experience."[83] This approach must inevitably, and will usually initially, alienate the conservative theologian from any serious dialogue with the social sciences, for, explains Berger, "conservative theology . . . tends to deduce from the tradition" whereas "liberal theology . . . tends to induce from generally accessible experience."[84] By this observation, Berger aligns himself with the attitude expressed earlier by Whitson to the effect that a challenge to a "theological formulation" is not a "challenge to the genuineness of the religious experience" which informs or supports the theological formulation, but rather is a challenge to the accuracy of the formulation in structuring an explanation of experience. Much undue resentment has resulted from a failure to articulate this difference. To differ over formulation is not tantamount to questioning one's religious integrity! The disputants in social science methodologies have seldom felt so.

Berger is calling for a revival of a "deeper motif" within theology characterized as the "Schleiermacher era" within which is "a spirit of patient induction and an attitude of openness to the fullness of human experience, especially as this experience is accessible to historical inquiry."[85] Having fully aligned himself with the liberal tradition, Berger then sets out to formulate what he considers to be the greatest challenge to that tradition which the social sciences have produced, viz., that of historical relativity.

> Only after the (liberal) theologian has confronted the historical relativity of religion can he genuinely ask where in this history it may, perhaps, be possible to speak of discoveries — discoveries that is, that transcend the relative charactaracter of their infrastructures. And only after he has really grasped what it means to say that religion is a human product . . . can be begin to search, within this array . . . for what may turn out to be signals of transcendence."[86]

The historical relativity of religion (and culture, too, for that matter), which Berger is addressing, seems to find similarity in Geertz's emphasis upon the historical transmission of culture and Tillich's notion of variety in form and content. A theology of experience must locate itself within this panorama of religious and cultural variety while at the same time addressing the systematics of religious phenomena. The relationship between the systematic analysis of socio-cultural structures and processes and the systematic analysis of religious expressions of meaning is possible according to Berger: "I strongly suspect that such an inquiry will . . . become an enterprise in anthropology . . . (A) theology that proceeds in a step-by-step correlation with what can be said about man empirically is well worth a serious try."[87]

From a sociological perspective, Berger has called for a beginning in the direction of dialogue. From an anthropological perspective, Whitson has taken the first crucial steps. "The formulation we seek," we quoted for Whitson earlier, "must arise from within actual religious experience."[88] Like Berger, Whitson posites the liberal approach to theological method, i.e., the recognition of human experience as the fundamental starting point for theology.[89] For Whitson, theology is understood to be an attempt to "analyze systematically the creative process in any religious tradition." Theology is, furthermore, "man in the process of knowing."[90] Being an anthropologist, Whitson attempts a construction of theological method which is cross-cultural, a comparative theology within which Christian, Muslim, Jewish, etc., theologies find points of commonality.[91] Religions for Whitson, as we noted earlier, are neither essentially alike nor are they necessarily mutually exclusive, present-day conservative theological polemic to the contrary notwithstanding.[92]

"The two basic elements, Man and Knowing," contends Whitson, "demand that any realistic theology be fully grounded in the historic character of religious tradition . . . (thus) the definition of theology we seek must be extended maximally and not derived from one tradition of religion or civilization."[93] This historico-cultural grounding is an answer to the plea of Berger cited earlier, and Whitson's quest for a theological method "extended maximally" is an effort to account for the imperative of man to understand his experience through its systematic analysis.[94] And, though every cultural and religious tradition does not intentionally engage in theology, no tradition is devoid of the experiential materials necessary for such a construction though possibly lacking in a sophisticated language of abstractions.[95] "Hence," continues Whitson, "both in content and function the logos-category must be treated as a logical abstraction . . . but must be located in the actual process of history."

The concern here, expressed by Whitson, is the construction of a method whereby the enterprise of "logical abstraction," i.e., the human interpretive element in theology called the logos-category, is complementary to an exmphasis upon the actual experience in human community. "If theology is to be situated in the actual condition of man," reasons Whitson, "and if the logos-category of theology is to reflect adequately man's experience of knowing, then the central recognition of theology must be . . . man (as) both individual and social, man communicating, man in an ultimately significant relationship."[96] Whitson is progressing toward his formal definition of theology by combining man's systematic analysis of religious experience with man's experience of himself as essentially a creature of relationships. Whitson defines religion "as man's relatedness in the sacred," — sacred here meaning man's experience of that relationship amidst other relationships which is ultimately significant or definitive. (This experience of man's "definitive relationship" is suggestive of Tillich's definition of religion as man being "grasped by his ultimate concern.") Whitson then defines theology as "the systematization of man's experience of definitive relationship."[97] Or, as we have been suggesting as a short-hand definition, theology is the systematics of religion.

Theology is systematic analysis of the actual human experience of that relationship which is Essential, Definitive, Ultimate. And, as religions arise (Whitson noted earlier), within communities during crises of meaning, we might suggest that theology is an analysis of that meaning which is viewed as Essential the expressions of which are existential, i.e., cultural. Theology, of course, can never fully delineate the Essential — it can only address it indirectly. Theology must, therefore, "deal with the fundamental paradox" (ineffability of the theos-category and the historicality of the logos-category) by "limiting its attempts to systematize to the observable relationship which actually occurs with the relativity of all others which guarantees that theology will remain oriented toward the full reality at the root of the experience even though it is inconceivable. Focused upon the definitiveness of the relationship, theology will also remain in communication with the rest of knowledge built around the attempt to articulate man's meaning."[98]

If theology is to remain open to dialogue with the social sciences, Whitson's suggestions must be elevated to directives, i.e., theology must systematize that part of the definitive relationship which is observable and be in consultation with the sciences of social observation and logic. In other words, while not forgetting the import of religion and its final ineffability, theology should continue to seriously seek out manifestations of this import, this experience of definitive relationship through cultural forms and contents. By so doing, a convergence of theological and anthropological methods are probable if not inevitable. Therefore, in view of these directives, Whitson points out three things "theology must do":

> First, since its disciplinary purpose is to systematize, it must be oriented to the objectivity of a tradition, to the analyzable content of its constitution. Next, the objective dimension must be accepted as occurring in subjective experience — sharing, and hence always in immediate positive relationship with all that the experiencer-sharers are, socially, culturally and psychologically (and therefore theology is necessarily and internally related to the empirical disciplines). Finally, as this religious community individually and together is necessarily processual, theology is always involved in and reflective of the creativity of the ongoing tradition. [99]

Geertz has set the stage for a convergence of anthropology and theology by venturing a definition of culture in terms of "meaning." Berger has advanced to center stage with a call for theology and the social sciences to engage seriously in dialogue. Whitson has begun the dialogue by constructing a definition and methodology for theology which is credible and promising from an anthropological perspective. Finally, Tillich, a philosopher of religion and theologian of culture has attempted to complete the dialogic circle by defining culture in a manner conducive to support from philosophy and theology, hoping in the end to give rise to a theological method of cultural analysis. Lest our ambitions become too flighty for sound reasoning, Heschel has registered a caution to those who would too easily conceptualize religious experience into systems: "The danger always exists of those moments (of experiential encounter with Essential Meaning) becoming distorted and even lost in the process of translation from situation to conceptualization."[100]

With the goal of dialogue and the caution of distortion firmly conjoined in our minds, let us draw this inquiry to a close with a brief consideration of Tillich's view of theological method and its relationship to cultural analysis. "Philosophy and theology (address) the question of being," Tillich says, explaining that "philosophy deals with the structure of being in itself; theology deals with the meaning of being for us."[101] Heidegger's influence upon the ontological structure of Tillich's philosophy of religion has already been mentioned.[102] More importantly for our interests is Tillich's characterization of theology as concerned with the "meaning of being for us." Through Tillich's method of "correlation,"[103] the ontological question of "being in itself" is answered from the existential question of the "meaning of being for us," i.e., philosophy asking and theology answering.

Theology is man's systematic attempt to answer the ontological question. Theology is generated out of actual human experience, and therefore, says Tillich, "the theological method (as he constructed it) . . . is a universal application of theological questioning to all cultural values." The universality of the theological method, suggested above by Whitson, is for Tillich a logical conclusion drawn from the universal questioning of man about "being" and its "meaning" for him.[104] "We have assigned to theology," continues Tillich, "the task of finding a systematic form of expression for a concrete religious standpoint."[105] The concreteness of the religious experience constitutes the fundamental focus of theology, as Whitson contended, in order for the logical abstraction of systematic analysis (theology) to speak to the human condition.

As anthropology begins with the experience in culture of existential meanings expressed in form and content, so likewise, theology begins with the experience in religion of Essential Meaning expressed in its import. "Our whole development of this theme," says Tillich, "has taken culture and its forms as a starting point and has shown how culture as such receives a religious quality when substance or import flow into form, and how it finally produces a specifically religious-cultural sphere in order to preserve and heighten that religious quality."[106] Theology is sytem, it is universally applicable, it is focused upon the ultimate concern of men as they express themselves in religious and cultural meaning-systems.

Tillich wrote extensively regarding the development of theological method, especially developed in the first volume of his SYSTEMATIC THEOLOGY. There were two formal criteria characteristic of his theological system: First, "The object of theology is what concerns us ultimately. Only those propositions are theological which deal with their object in so far as it can become a matter of ultimate concern for us." Second, "Our ultimate concern is that which determines our being or not-being. Only those statements are theological which deal with their object in so far as it can become a matter of being or not-being for us."[107] These two criteria must characterize every theological method and system if those methods and systems are understood to be the systematization of religious experience.

It is the theology of culture within the systematic theology of Tillich which is of special importance to us, for "the theology of culture," explains Tillich, "is the attempt to analyze the theology behind all cultural expression, to discover the ultimate concern . . . "[108] No cultural expression is without a religious substance though the cultural expression's intention is not religious as such. A theology of culture is a systematic analysis of the substance of culture in an attempt to discover culture's religious core (Buber and Heschel have spoken of the discoverability of meaning vis a vis Nietzsche and Sartre who spoke of creating meaning.)

A theology of culture must be established upon a well-developed systematics wherein the method of correlation, i.e., philosophy asking and theology answering, informs the theologizing process, according to Tillich. But also, a genuine theology of culture must be substantially informed by and in touch with its own culture — its moods and styles. Tillich, being a noteworthy historian of art and a recognized art critic, understood the interplay in his own life of the theological and the aesthetical.[109] As Tillich's theology of culture grows out of his systematic theology, so necessarily his systematics is centered in actual human experiences of meaning which seek for religious and cultural expressions. "The sources of systematic theology," says Tillich, "can be sources only for one who participates in them, that is, through experience."[110]

A theology of culture seeks for the theological infrastructure of all cultural expressions, and wherever culture expresses itself, a theology of culture has its task laid out. "The task of a theology of culture," explains Tillich, "is to follow up . . . all the spheres and creations of culture and to give it (the theology behind culture) expressions."[111] Of course, theology has its own agenda, and is not designed to encroach upon other methods of cultural analysis but rather seeks to sit among the various methods with equal privilege. Theology's approach is "not from the standpoint of form," explains Tillich, for "that would be the task of the branch of cultural science concerned — but taking the import or substance as its starting point, as theology of culture and not as cultural systematization."[112] The distinction is crucial — that between cultural systematization of form (anthropology) and the systematic analysis of import (theology) — for otherwise we would have the very discipline which we wish to engage in dialogue engaged in competitive interpretations.

Unless the distinctions are held constant between form/content and import, our efforts will fail. Tillich is attempting to develop a theology which would be considered "a normative science of religion" — our term explains this as the "systematics of religion," and Whitson has even suggested "theology of religion." "The concrete religious experiences embedded in all great cultural phenomena," suggests Tillich, "must be brought into relief and a mode of expression found for them."[113] And therefore, what is needed and that for which Tillich labored was, in addition to a normative science of religion focused upon the universal religious experiences of men embedded in cultural phenomena, a theological method which could stand beside systematic theology "in the same way that a psychological and a sociological method, etc., exist alongside systematic psychology."[114]

CONCLUSION . . .

Our effort has been to demonstrate the possibility of a positive dialogue between the social sciences (especially anthropology) and theology (especially liberal theology from Schleiermacher). Beginning with a current definition of culture as "patterns of meanings" (Geertz) and religion as "man's encounter with the meaning of being" (Tillich), we have worked through these meaning-systems to their systematic analysis, defining anthropology as the "systematics of culture" and theology as the "systematics of religion."

The possibilities for mutual interaction between the social sciences and theology are hopefully made clearer. The outgrowth in such a dialogue (called for by Berger and begun by Whitson) are provocatively diverse: First, such a dialogue should begin to dispel antipathy and usher in a cordial and consultative atmosphere between these two disciplines, each carrying out the analysis of meaning-systems within the scope of its methodology while consulting with the other at crucial points of convergence, e.g., myth and symbol. Second, in such a dialogue, theology could become increasingly informed of and sensitive to the vast range of human religious experience found in anthropology while anthropology could increase its own insights into religio-cultural analysis under the influence of a theological method addressed to the import of meaning-systems. As demonstrated by Whitson, a third outgrowth would hopefully be a more substantially developed theological method addressed to the diversity of formulations of Essential Meaning whereby a dialogue between the world religions might prove creative, i.e., away from suspicion and toward understanding.

BIBLIOGRAPHY

1. Clifford Geertz, "Ethos, World-View and the Analysis of Sacred Symbols," Antioch Review (Winter, 1957-58), 436.

2. Susan K. Langer, Philosophical Sketches (New York: Mentor, 1964), p. 54.

3. As quoted in Martin Buber, Between Man and Man (New York: Macmillan, 1968), p. 182.

4. Abraham J. Heschel, Who Is Man? (Stanford: University Press, 1968), p. 50.

5. Ibid., p. 51.

6. Ibid., p. 52.

7. Geertz, "Ethos, World-View . . . ", p. 422.

8. Among the most important functionalists, Durkheim and Weber stand as the grand masterbuilders, followed by Malinowski, Radcliffe-Brown, Homans and Wallace. The scope of functionalists' aspirations is summed up by Malinowski: "The functional method stands and falls with the possibility of defining the whole of the supernatural." "Anthropology," in Encyclopaedia Britannica, supplementary volume 29: 131-140.

9. Clifford Geertz, "Religion as a Cultural System," in Michael Banton (ed.), Anthropological Approaches to the Study of Religion (London: Tavstock, 1968), p. 3.

10. Major textbook examples include: Conrad Phillip Kottak, Anthropology: The Exploration of Human Diversity (New York: Random House, 1974), p. 492; "Culture — behavior patterns acquired by humans as members of society";

William A. Haviland, Anthropology (New York: Holt, Rinehart, and Winston, 1974), p. 8: "When we speak of culture, we refer to man's learned behavior . . . Culture is the way of life of an entire people."

11. Robley Edward Whitson, The Coming Convergence in World Religion, (New York: Newman Press, 1971), p. 8.

12. Ibid., p. 10.

13. Paul Tillich, What Is Religion? (New York: Harper Torchbook, 1969), pp. 22, 19.

14. Ibid., p. 57.

15. "The word 'meaning,' of course, is not unambiguous. But the merely logical use of the term ('a word has a meaning') is transcended if one speaks of 'life in meanings.' If the term 'meaning' is used in this sense, one should describe the production of the new in history as the production of new and unique embodiments of meaning. My preference for this latter terminology is based partly on the rejection of the anti-ontological value theory and partly on the importance of terms like 'the meaning of life' for philosophy of religion. A phrase like 'the value of life' has neither the depth nor the breadth of 'the meaning of life'." Paul Tillich, Systematic Theology (Chicago: University Press, 1967), III: 304.

16. Tillich, What Is Religion?, p. 57.

17. Geertz, "Religion as a Cultural System," p. 3.

18. Cf. my article, "Religious Myth and Symbol: A Convergence of Philosophy and Anthropology," Philosophy Today, XVIII, 4 (Spring, 1974), 68-84. This essay is an inquiry into the importance of the philosophy of myth and symbol as found in the works of Ernst Cassirer, Paul Ricoeur, and Philip Wheelwright to symbolic anthropology.

19. Susan K. Langer, Philosophy in a New Key (New York: Mentor, 1951), p. 55.

20. Ibid., p. 56.

21. Ibid., p. 64.

22. Geertz, "Religion as a Cultural System," p. 8.

23. Langer, Philosophical Sketches, p. 60.

24. Langer, Philosophy in a New Key, p. 90.

25. I. C. Jarvis, The Revolution in Anthropology (Chicago: Henry Regnery, 1969). This is a serious attempt at a philosophical critique of anthropological methodology.

26. Clifford Geertz, "Ritual and Social Change: A Javanese Example," in William A. Lessa and Evon Z. Vogt, Reader in Comparative Religion: An Anthropological Approach (New York: Harper and Row, 1965, second edition), p. 549.

27. Ibid., p. 549.

28. "It is the thesis of this paper," begins Geertz, "that one of the major reasons for the inability of functional theory to cope with change lies in its failure to treat sociological and cultural process on equal terms; almost inevitably one of the two is either ignored or is sacrificed to become but a simple reflex, a mirror of image, of the others . . . (A) revision of the concepts of functional theory . . . begins with an attempt to distinguish analytically between the cultural and social aspects of human life, and to treat them as independently variable yet mutually interdependent factors." Ibid., p. 548.

29. Langer, Philosophical Sketches, p. 87.

30. Heschel, Who Is Man?, p. 55.

31. Ibid., p. 54.

32. Ibid.

33. Ibid., p. 55.

34. Ibid., p. 67.

35. Tillich, Systematic Theology, III: 84.

36. Clifford Geertz, The Interpretation of Cultures: Selected Essays (New York: Basic Books, 1973), pp. 5, 29.

37. The social scientific study of religion has produced near countless definitions of religion as well as a baffling number of legitimate, quasi-, and pseudo-methodologies for the study of religion. Geertz's criticism of the insufficiency of a functionalist definition and methodology has been similarly heard from Wach in earlier days. "Those of us who study the sociological implications of religion will err if we imagine that our work will reveal the nature and essence of religion itself." Joachim Wach, Sociology of Religion (Chicago: University Press, 1944), p. 4, and more recently from Bellah: "Much of social science has relapsed into the positivist, utilitarian idiom in which only 'hard and realistic' assumptions about nature are allowed. In this idiom, human action is likened to a game where every player is trying to maximize his self interest or is concerned only with the quid pro quo in an exchange network . . . Religion for these of this persuasion could hardly be less important, or if its survival is recognized, it is explained away as a response to some sort of deprivation . . . (Such) views are . . . convenient, for they fit the governing myth in which the world is seen as a highly complex machine entirely subject to rational calculation," Robert Bellah, Beyond Belief (New York: Harper and Row, 1970), p. 241.

38. With Thomas Luckmann, Peter Berger has done a pioneering work in American theoretical sociology with their The Social Construction of Reality (Garden City: Doubleday, 1967).

39. Peter Berger, A Rumor of Angels: Modern Society and the Rediscovery of the Sacred (New York: Anchor, 1970), p. 46.

40. Peter Berger, The Sacred Canopy: Elements of a Sociological Theory of Religion (New York: Anchor, 1970), p. 48.

41. A profound treatment from the point of view of phenomenology of religion has been done by G. Van Der Leeuw, Religion in Essence and Manifestation: A STudy in Phenomenology (New York: Harper and Row, 1963, 2 volumes).

42. "The most convincing and far-reaching attempt to define religion in terms of its social functionality is that of Thomas Luckmann, The Invisible Religion, 1967 . . . (T)he essence of Luckmann's conception of religion is the capacity of the human organism to transcend its biological nature through constructions of objective, morally binding, all-embracing universe of meaning . . . I question the utility of a definition that equates religion with the human tout court . . . I have tried . . . to operate with a substantive definition of religion in terms of the positing of a sacred cosmos." Berger, The Sacred Canopy, pp. 176-177.

43. Ibid., p. 180.

44. Geertz, "Religion as a Cultural System," p. 5.

45. J. Milton Yinger, The Scientific Study of Religion (New York: Macmillan, 1970), p. 7.

46. Geertz, "Religion as a Cultural System," p. 14.

47. Ibid., p. 24.

48. Ibid., p. 25.

49. William Cenkner, review of Whitson's The Coming Convergence of World Religions, Cross Currents, XXII, 3 (Winter, 1973), 429-437.

50. Whitson, The Coming Convergence, p. x.

51. Ibid., p. 3.

52. Ibid., p. 8.

53. "If I have done away with God the Father," Sartre says literally, "someone is needed to invent values . . . Life has no meaning a priori . . . (I)t is up to you to give it meaning, and value is nothing else than this meaning which you choose," L'Existentialisme Est Un Humanisme, 1964, p. 89. Buber in an essay entitled, "Religion and Modern Thinking," has responded to Sartre in this manner: "One can believe in and accept a meaning or value . . . if one has discovered it, not if one has invented it. It can be for me an illuminating meaning, a direction giving value, only if it has been revealed to me in my meeting with being, not if I have freely chosen it for myself from among the existing possibilities . . . " As quoted in Buber, Between Man and Man, p. 199.

54. Whitson, The Coming Convergence, p. 10.

55. Tillich, What Is Religion?, p. 19.

56. "The unconditioned meaningfulness of all meaning depends upon the awareness of the inexhaustibility of meaning in the ground of meaning." Ibid., p. 58.

57. Ibid., p. 19.

58. Cf. my article "Theology and Symbol: An Anthropological Approach," Journal of Religious Thought, XXX, 2 (Fall-Winter, 1973-74), 51-61.

59. Tillich, What Is Religion?, p. 20.

60. "The living dialectic of the elements of meaning (i.e., of form and import) . . . penetrates the whole of reality." Ibid., p. 50.

61. "This import of meaning," explains Adams, "is most readily observable in a painting wherein it is suffused by a quality that breaks through the form and content." Ibid.

62. Ibid.

63. Ibid.

64. Paul Tillich, Theology of Culture (Oxford: University Press, 1968), p. 42.

65. Tillich, What Is Religion?, p. 59. Reminiscent of Heschel's statement cited earlier, Tillich says, "Every cultural act contains the unconditioned meaning . . . (and therefore) culture as culture is substantially, but not intentionally, religiou." Ibid.

66. Ibid., pp. 60, 66.

67. Tillich, Systematic Theology, III: 84.

68. Culture as "the historically transmitted pattern of meanings embodied in a complex of symbols" is pursued extensively in Geertz's analysis of symbol in his essay, "Ethos, World-View and the Analysis of Sacred Symbols," cited earlier, in which he says, " . . . meanings can only be 'stored' in symbols . . . " Tillich has pursued the analysis of the religious symbol in his essay, "The Religious Symbol," found in Daedalus: Journal of the American Academy of Arts and Science, LXXXVII, 3 (Summer, 1958), 3-21, in which he says the religious symbol is "a representation of that which is unconditionally beyond the conceptual sphere, they point to the ultimate reality in the religious act, to what concerns us ultimately."

69. Cf. my "Theology and Symbol . . . " in the Journal of Religious Thought.

70. Geertz, "Religion as a Cultural System," p. 42.

71. "The concept of culture I espouse," explains Geertz, "and whose utility the essays below attempt to demonstrate, is essentially a semiotic one. Believing, with Max Weber, that man is an animal suspended in webs of significance he himself has spun, I take culture to be those webs, and the analysis of it to be therefore not an experimental science in search of law but an interpretive one in search of meaning . . . Meaning, that elusive and ill-defined pseudoentity we were once more than content to leave philosophers and literary critics to fumble with, has now come back into the heart of our discipline." Geertz, The Interpretation of Cultures, pp. 5, 29.

72. Ibid., p. 9.

73. Ibid., p. 14.

74. Ibid., p. 30. "Nothing is more necessary to comprehending what anthropological interpretation is, and the degree to which it is interpretation, than an exact understanding of what it means — and what it does not mean — to say that our formulations of other people's symbol systems must be actor-oriented." Ibid., p. 14.

75. In Geertz's article, "Religion as a Cultural System," he has treated the nature and relationship of worldview (structure of reality — metaphysics) and ethos (style of life — values), demonstrating how that sacred symbols "function to synthesize" these two elements within the religious community.

76. Berger, The Sacred Canopy, p. 22. "One fundamental human trait, which is of crucial importance in understanding man's religious enterprise," Berger says in another place, "is his propensity for order." Berger, A Rumor of Angels, p. 53.

77. An ethnographic confirmation of this human trait is classically demonstrated in Paul Radin's Primitive Man as Philosopher (New York: Dover, 1957). In the Preface (p. xxi) Radin says, "There can be little doubt that every group, no matter how small, has, from time immemorial, contained individuals who were constrained by their individual temperaments to occupy themselves with the basic problems of what we customarily term philosophy."

78. The term "culture," so central to the discipline of anthropology, has been defined in numerous ways. In addition to those mentioned in footnote 10 above, cf. also a list of definitions in Charles Winick, Dictionary of Anthropology (Totowa, New Jersey: Littlefield, Adams, 1968).

79. The term "theology" has had a long history of disputed definitions as to its nature and task, and time does not allow of a survey. However, a considerable diversity of definitions now exists between Thomists, Barthians, Liberals, and Radicals.

80. "In a very real sense," says Berger, "neo-orthodoxy in its original impulse, was anti-anthropological. In other words, an anthropology could be theologically deduced, but there was no inductive possibilities from anthropology to theology. (Barth's "no" to the Catholic analogia entis — "analogy of being" between God and Man — makes that clear) . . . (T)he Swiss theologian, Emil Brunner . . . represented the modification of the neo-orthodox aversion to anthropological consideration . . . (in) what he called the problem of the anknupfungspunkt — the "point of contact" between God's revelation and the human situation." Berger, A Rumor of Angels, p. 50.

81. Paul L. Holmer, Theology and the Scientific Study of Religion (Minneapolis: T. S. Denison, 1961). This constitutes a theologian's attempt to speak to the social sciences, but from the standpoint of the social sciences is not a serious effort in setting up grounds for serious dialogue.

82. Berger, A Rumor of Angels, p. 52.

83. Ibid., p. 57.

84. Ibid., p. 76.

85. Ibid., p. 82.

86. Berger, The Sacred Canopy, p. 185. In another place, a comparative study of Berger's "signals of transcendence" and Tillich's "import of religion" might prove most provocative.

87. Ibid., p. 185.

88. Whitson, The Coming Convergence, p. x.

89. "The issue," says Whitson, "is to come to a definition of theology, not simply as an abstraction but as an expression of the human experience, as a reality lived out by actual men, and thus as significant within the context of the human situaion." Robley Edward Whitson, "The Situation of Theology," in F. J. Jurji (ed.) Religious Pluralism and World Community: Interfaith and Intercultural Communication (Leiden: E. J. Brill, 1969). In this essay, Whitson analyzes theology in terms of its constituent elements, i.e., theos — that category of ultimate ineffability constituting the core of religious experience which transcends the capacity of intellectual comprehension and must be experientially apprehended, and logos — the uniquely human realm of intellectual reflection and formulation.

90. Whitson, The Coming Convergence, pp. 59, 67.

91. Whitson has suggested that "the actual conceptual content (of a theological system) is not valid simply because the religious experiences (are) valid . . . The variety in theological expression must be accounted for by the range of materials which go to form the consciousness of the individual . . . (and furthermore) the validity of the religious experience and hence of the recognition of mystery, ineffability, does not depend upon the way in which it is conceived . . . (A) theory advanced to provide an understanding of observed experience cannot be valid if it first calls for the denial of the data supposedly being studied. (And finally), theology as a process of knowledge dealing with religious experience in the context of an identifiable tradition does not deal with the theos-category directly but only relationally." ibid., pp. 108-111.

92. Of equal problematic to attempts at genuine religious dialogue to the conservatives are those liberals who assume that all religions are finally alike, and therefore differences are unimportant. This so-called liberal perspective may, after all, be more dangerous in dialogue than the conservative approach.

93. Whitson, The Coming Convergence, p. 59.

94. Cf. my discussion of homo interpres in "Religious Myth and Symbol."

95. Whitson has demonstrated the possibilities for a theological method of this design in a stimulating analysis of the teachings of Confucius. Cf. Herbert Fingarette, Confucius: The Secular as Sacred (New York: Harper Torchbook, 1972), for a treatment of the religious dynamic within Confucianism.

96. Whitson, The Coming Convergence, p. 67.

97. Ibid., p. 113.

98. Ibid., p. 114.

99. Ibid., p. 56.

100. Heschel, Who Is Man?. p. 2.

101. Tillich, Systematic Theology, I:22.

102: "The ontological approach to philosophy of religion . . . is able to . . . overcome as far as it is possible by mere thought the fateful gap between religion and culture, thus reconciling concerns which are not strange to each other but have been estranged from each other." Tillich, Theology of Culture, p. 29.

103. The concept of "correlation" is central to Tillich's philosophy of religion and theology and has been discussed in numerous places, a good example being an essay by George F. Thomas, "The Method and Structure of Tillich's Theology," in Charles W. Kegley and Robert W. Bretall (eds.), The Theology of Paul Tillich (New York: Macmillan, 1961).

104. "Schleiermacher's 'feeling of absolute dependence' was rather near to what is called in the present system 'ultimate concern about the ground and meaning of our being'." Tillich, Systematic Theology, I: 42. Tillich often voiced his indebtedness to Schleiermacher and Schelling for their impact upon his system with regard to the construction of a theological method addressed to experience.

105. Tillich, What Is Religion?. p. 165.

106. A perennial danger which Tillich saw was the unceasing attempt of both religious and secular forms and contents laying claim to the "possession of the sacred" instead of "conveying the sacred" through its agencies. "The whole work of

theology," concluded Tillich in speaking of this danger, "can be summed up in the statement, that it is the permanent guardian of the unconditional against the aspiration of its own religious and secular appearances . . . " Tillich, Theology of Culture, p. 29.

107. Tillich, Systematic Theology, I: 12, 14.

108. Ibid., I: 39.

109. "The key to the theological understanding of a cultural creation," said Tillich, "is its style. Style is a term derived from the realm of the arts, but it can be applied to all realms of culture . . . " Ibid., I: 40.

110. Ibid.

111. Tillich, What Is Religion?, p. 164.

112. Ibid.

113. Ibid.

114. Ibid.

CHAPTER SIX

"Maritime Canadians and the Quest for Meaning,"

Ann Marie Powers
SUNY — Stony Brook

In a collection of seminal essays Clifford Geertz presents a symbolic interpretation of culture and society which serves to illustrate how functionalist explanations of the social order, while useful in understanding particular social relationships, social institutions and rituals, often do not provide a complete picture of the way these social relationships or rituals shape the social order and are in turn shaped by it.[1] The focus of this essay is certainly not to refute functionalist analyses, but rather to apply Geertz's theoretical suggestions, i.e., construct "a reading of what happens" to a custom which is still quite widespread throughout the Canadian Province of Newfoundland and Labrador — Christmas mummering or janneying.[2] Although mummers are present today in Newfoundland, according to some sources it is on the decline due to increasing industrialization and the concommitant increased contact local peoples in isolated settlements (outports) have with 'outsiders'. It is the purpose of the article to present a symbolic interpretation of Newfoundland mummers and to demonstrate how mummering does and will continue in the future to fit into "the fabric of meaning" of Newfoundland culture and society.[3]

Christmas mummering and false faces

The practice or art of masking, putting on costumes and disguises and the presence of frightening figures in pivotal rituals is well documented in the anthropological, historical and folkloric literature. Indeed, Christmas mummering in the form of the house visit dates back to the early 1800's and in accordance with Newfoundland history, reportedly originated in the British Isles.[4] In Newfoundland mummering occurs during the twelve days of Christmas, December 26-January 6. Although mummers make house calls every night during the Christmastide, it is on and after the night of January 1st that the mummers' visits become more intensified and frequent. Such visits, especially by adults, occur most often after midnight.[5] The mummers usually gather in groups of two or more each night; however, a person will often change the people with whom he'll mummer from night to night so as to better conceal his/her identity from those whose house is entered for a visit several nights in succession. If the people in the house guess the identity of one mummer, it often leads them to attempt and correctly guess the identity of the others. Since people generally mummer along kinship, residential or friendship lines, changing partners is part of the disguise and hence part of the ritual.

Mummers meet at the house of one of the group and disguise themselves by putting on old clothing or wrapping sheets and muslin around them. Men sometimes dress up as women and women disguise themselves as males, wearing the fishing gear of oil skins, rubbers and mitts. The mummer's face is blackened or covered with a veil, fastened securely, in order to be sure to conceal it. They change their 'gait' (the mummers walk) and, if possible, their height (by slouching over or adding stuffing inside their boots to lift themselves higher). Most of all the mummers disguise their voices in what is known as 'mummer talk,' whereby the speech of a particular person cannot be identified. Mummer talk is a garbled speech, which is spoken while breathing in, talking quickly and in a different tone of voice. This ingressive speech pattern, when mastered, is considered by many to be a sure sign of a good mummer. Many times only one or two of the mummers in a group will be the spokesmen for all, as they might be considered the best at disguising their voices. Indeed, I myself was told that if I went mummering, I would have to be a silent mummer, since it was considered that I would be unable to speak mummer talk and would probably give myself and those accompanying me away almost immediately.

The final part of the disguise is the 'split' of wood which is carried around and used to knock on the doors of the houses to be visited while asking 'mummers allowed?' This request is often made more than once before the mummers are permitted to enter. If the hosts do not wish to have the mummers come in they will not respond to the knocking at the door. The knock at the door is important to keep in mind in discussing the ritual of the mummers. As anyone who has ever lived in the outports of Newfoundland soon learns, one does not knock upon entering a house for a visit. It is only strangers who will knock on the door, but surely no one from the settlement who is known, a friend, or a kinsman from elsewhere. It is only recently that one finds members of a settlement knocking at the door, and then it is usually children who are selling vegetables or papers from door-to-door. The knocking, as James Faris notes, is indicative of an outside relationship – it is something new and out of the ordinary.[6] "A person in the community who wishes to establish one of these 'stranger-like' relationships will signal this by knocking, just as the outsider and the mummer do."[7] Another significant aspect of the preparations is that no one talks about going mummering. It is understood that mummers will visit at some time, but is an unspoken of event which is often anxiously awaited.

The usual daily house visit is a very common pattern in Newfoundland during the year, but moreso at Christmas. Women prepare for Christmas by baking fruit cakes, sweet bread and biscuits. Men prepare by having some alcoholic beverages to serve. During the summer it is the women who do most of the visiting, as the men are out fishing. When the men do get together it is usually in one of the local small shops or at the local 'club' (commonly a branch of the Royal Canadian Legion). During Christmas, however, and particularly after Midnight Mass, both men and women will visit close kin and partying and visiting will continue all through the night and throughout the twelve days of Christmas.

As mentioned above, the appearance and/or anticipation of mummers is not spoken of at all. People walk in and out of the house, sit down to talk and visit in the kitchen, which is the room where most of the daily life of the family goes on during the year, and will imbibe in some drinking. If a loud knock suddenly comes to the door accompanied by a cry of 'mummers allowed?', the household falls silent. If the mummers are allowed in, they will be greeted with a reply of 'mummers allowed, come on in', or someone goes to the door to let them in. In many ways the mummers are treated as invited guests. Once they enter a house the mummers will be invited to sit down. The spokesman will talk with the host and some of the mummers will be questioned. They may be asked to dance or perform in some way (give a recitation or sing). If they oblige, the mummers try to imitate the step of another so as to confuse the host and the others present and thus prevent their being able to unravel the mummers' true identity. It must be remembered that in small, farily isolated settlements people often know each other by their 'gait' or certain other traits they might possess; hence the mummers disguise is to hide their own identity and mimic that of another. There are times when mummers would use the opportunity of being disguised to grumble or be hostile, but this was not what I found to be the case and seems to have been infrequent.[8] In most reports of such activities the disturbances were during the mummers parade, which is a separate event from the mummers house visit discussed herein; and such parades in which hostilities did break out were mostly those held in and around the City of St. John's, the capital of the Province.[9]

There are three essential aspects of the mummers visits which are important in interpreting this ritual: the 'false face,' the knock at the door, and the time of the year in which mummering takes place, as well as the time of their arrival for a house visit. The 'false face' is perhaps the most significant aspect of the disguise as it not only conceals an individual's identity, but is designed to deceive the host and his guests. A person's face is hidden under a veil or else blackened to accomplish this objective. Since Newfoundland outporters frown upon strangers, especially those whom they consider to be 'black ones' or 'black strangers' (someone whom they do not know at all nor have any knowledge about, either in terms of their kinship or ethnic ties), the mummers fulfill this function. They are indeed 'black ones'. The ritual knock at the door is also important, as it is only strangers who are known to knock. Just as in-depth inquiries are made to learn something about an 'outsider' or stranger in the settlement, so too, the host to a group of mummers will question them to try and unravel the mystery of the masked visitors and ascertain their identity. Third, to fully understand mummering it must be understood within the context in which it occurs. Most Newfoundlanders fear the dark and do not like to travel alone when night falls. The mummers only visit at night, usually after midnight, i.e., during a transitional phase. Further, it is a ritual which occurs at a liminal time of the year — the trnasition to the New Year.[10] Just as strangers are in a liminal state, the same holds true for the mummers. Both are questioned, prodded and given hospitality to learn more about them. They are indeed marginal figures.

When and if a mummer is properly identified, he and those with him may or may not reveal their identities. But more often than not they do make themselves known. In either case the mummers are offered food and drink and then they will leave. But it should be noted that if their identity is not guessed and remains unknown, the mummers leave rather quickly after having a drink or some food. Sometimes the mummers may even tell their host where they will go next. Once the mummers leave there is much discussion on how much fun the group of mummers happened to be and also speculation as to how well the next host will do in ascertaining the identity of the mummers. Sometimes those present will talk about the superb disguises and of how much they were fooled. Inevitably the cause of most of the conversation when the mummers leave is focused upon those who left without being definitely identified. Then those present will boast about how they know who it was all along, but didn't want to spoil the fun, and proceed to talk about how good they often were in the past in guessing the identities of the mummers.

When the mummers leave a house they will often boast of their own disguises and of how good they were at keeping their 'false face.' Sometimes they will admonish one another for 'giving them away' or else command each other on their performances in fooling their hosts. If they should meet up with other mummers, the groups may split. Again, this is to confuse the hosts, as at the end of a night some mummers may return to a house which they had visited earlier. It has been known for husbands and wives to go back to their own houses fooling each other.[11]

As noted, there have been cases where mummers were known to become boisterous and, at times, fighting broke out between them on the roads and pathways. But such fighting was rare and most of it took place between Catholics and Protestants living near each other.[12] For the most part, however, such activities are now uncommon. In the vicinity where I conducted my investigations there was one settlement which was dispersed over a coastline for approximately three miles. Since many of the women from 'up' and 'down' the harbour, respectively, do not see each other throughout the year because there is much to be done within the household during the fishery and little time for a lengthy visit, it seems that mummers who reside up the harbour will go mummering down the harbour and vice-versa. The mummers feel their identity is less likely to be revealed very quickly in such cases. The same does not seem to hold for the routine Christmas house visiting, however, as most of these follow close kinship and residential lines.

The Inshore Fishery and the Role of Affines and Strangers

A brief examination of the inshore (small trap crew) fishery in Newfoundland will enable us to grasp a better understanding not only of the mummers visits, but the daily house visits during the year, and the Christmastide visiting.

The Island of Newfoundland, with a population of approximately a little over one-half million, has been characterized by diversity ever since it was first settled by West Country English, Irish and French in the 16th-18th Centuries. According to local myths, and also several noted sources, the settlements in Newfoundland are so isolated because the sites were deliberately chosen in order to hide from the English and French merchants and military, the former of whom made permanent settlement illegal in the early 17th Century.[13] C. Grant Head, a geographer, and Ralph Matthews, an anthropologist, both refute this claim.[14] Head argues that settlement sites were chosen on the basis of ecological advantages; i.e., fishermen learned to locate those areas that would provide good fishing, as well as furnish protection from winter storms and floods. The result, no matter which explanation one accepts, is that settlements are quite far apart and many are still inaccessible by roads. Consequently, the coastal fishing outports, having a history of limited and restricted contact with other settlements, are today still largely self-sufficient and self-reliant in social and interpersonal relationships, although they are closely linked with the larger, national economy for trade and supplies.[15] To some extent it may perhaps be said that it is a combination of the isolation and the historical conditions existing at the time of early settlements which enabled the ritual of mummering to begin and persist in Newfoundland, and which accounted for what has been often referred to as the 'stranger complex' in the Province of Newfoundland and Labrador.[16] Mummering at Christmas not only describes the social order, but continually shapes it. As for strangers, one often hears the comment that 'you don't know who they are or what they might do.' This is also the case with mummers and generally is the reason given by a host who hesitates to invite them in and/or will admit them only after persistence on the part of the Mummers. Some people will not allow the mummers to enter their home at all, just as they will not invite a real stranger into their home until more is known about them.

The small inshore fishing crews in Newfoundland consist ideally of fathers and sons or a group of brothers, and it is the males who inherit land and fishing gear from their father. Thomas Nemec refers to this as impartible inheritance by the male sibling set, i.e., the sons inherit the fishing gear collectively and equally.[17] Land is inherited individually, each brother receiving a separate but equal parcel of land upon marriage. It is usually the youngest son who inherits the father's house and land. Hence in most Newfoundland outports we find a patrilocal residency rule and brothers living adjacent to each other. This grouping of the patrilocal extended family thus has a territorial and kinship designation.[18] The males ideally are involved in a common economic endeavor, e.g., fishing, and the families share one or adjoining gardens. As for fishing, affines are clearly not the first choice in the formation of fishing crews[19] and although in most Newfoundland outports there are local rules of exogamy based upon residency and surname, marriages to local women are preferred as women (and men) from other settlements are considered as outsiders, i.e., strangers. As Faris notes for Cat Harbour, men advised their sons not to marry a woman who was too far away — not to marry a stranger as "you can't trust them!"[20]

Mummers and Strangers — Interpretive Play in Outport Newfoundland

In a collection of essays by several anthropologists and folklorists entitled Christmas Mumming in Newfoundland, several explanations are postulated to account for the mummer complex: e.g., that it serves as a form of social control since children especially are often frightened and threatened by mummers and/or by strangers.[21] Indeed, it is not unusual for women to admonish their children with the comment that 'the mummers' or 'the boo man' or 'the stranger' will take them away if they are not good.[22] Another reason put forth is that mummering and its sometime accompanying aggressive play is a psychological mechanism to release hostility and in-group aggression.[23] In 1976 Gerald Sider presented a Marxist analysis to explain the rise, spread and what he sees as a decline of mummering in Newfoundland and Labrador.[24] He attributes the decrease in mummering to the decline of the inshore "family-based fishery" and therefore, its function to reproduce the relations of production by reaffirming kinship ties has creased, as it is no longer necessary. I do not disagree with Sider's explanation as his analysis is a cogent one and supports some of my own observations. However, his statement regarding the decline of the inshore fishery is too general and becomes questionable on the basis of the existing ethnographic data. But as with the other explanations offered, it is apparent that Sider, likewise, does not tell us much about what mummers themselves are. Following James C. Faris, who picks up on some of Melvin Firestone's ideas, it appears that to understand the ritual of mummering and the whole mumming complex is to understand Newfoundland society and culture. Firestone argues for the functional equivalence between mummers and strangers but adds that he does not want to imply that the people "consciously feel that mummers symbolize strangers . . . "[25] Faris, on the other hand, thinks Firestone has made a clear case for the conceptual similarities between the two and feels that "the cognition of the stranger, symbolized in the mummer, has rather wide and significant structural implications."[26] For Faris, the stranger falls into a category of persons whom outport Newfoundlanders generally fear and of whom they are wary. Hence, Faris argues, when local people go mummering and take on their disguises they adopt what he refers to as a sanctioned role reversal which enables them, in their polluted state, to take on the attributes of strangers.[27] To carry the argument a step further, it seems to this observer that if we look more closely at the ethnographic data we will see that there is no need to look for the behavior which might mark the stranger. Mummers do not merely symbolize strangers. What sets mummering apart as a ritual which both shapes and is shaped by the social order is that mummers are strangers.

To paraphrase Geertz, the whole mumming complex is "a metasocial commentary" upon the way in which Newfoundland society sorts its people and then organizes "the major part of collective existence around that assortment."[28] Mummering is a Newfoundland reading of their own experiences " . . . a story they tell themselves about themselves."[29] Mummering is not so much a practice to reaffirm the social relations of production or a catharsis for the release of hostilities. There are many ways in which every day behavior and activity serve these normative functions, especially in the Newfoundlanders behavior towards affines — their virtual exclusion from fishing crews and inheritance; the accusations of witchcraft made against affines, in particular women; and the general curiosity over strangers, particularly 'black strangers.'[30] Affines are only one category in a whole paradigm of strangers which influence and demonstrate the way Newfoundland society is structured and organized. While most mummers do eventually reveal themselves, there are cases where certain ones have remained unknown for some time. Although the facade of mummers and most 'real' strangers is eventually revealed, the latter will continue to occupy that category no matter how long they live in a settlement and how many people get to know them.

Although mummering is declining somewhat among adults, the ritual continues and can be seen as both a response to and a reaffirmation of considering outsiders as strangers. Since 1949 and Confederation with Canada many Newfoundland settlements have become more accessible to the outside and to neighboring outports. Such access has brought the outporter into contact with strangers almost daily, especially in the summer months when many campers and some tourists travel throughout the Province. Although such contact may be brief and limited, it is no longer an occasional event. Adults deal with outsiders and have come to expect them with more frequency; yet the comment will often be heard that 'there are a lot of strangers around this year.' Mummers are strangers who occupy the realm of the sacred. As such their behavior during the twelve days of Christmas is sanctioned and expected. Real strangers, those who belong to the profane sphere of daily life, are very much a part of the social order and hence occupy an important category in Newfoundland society. Consequently, both strangers and mummers will continue to be a part of Newfoundland culture and society in the future.

NOTES

1. Clifford Geertz, The Interpretation of Cultures (New York: Basic Books, 1973).

2. Ibid., p. 18. Fieldwork upon which the following article is based was conducted 14 months, 1976-1979. I would like to thank Dr. John Phalen, Dr. Pedro Carrasco and Prof. David Hicks for their comments. The research was supported by the Dept. of Anthropology, SUNY Stony Brook; The Institute of Social and Economic Research, Memorial University of Newfoundland; and the Arctic Institute of North America with the financial assistance of the Firestone Foundation.

3. Ibid., p. 145.

4. Herbert Halpert, "A Typology of Mumming," in Christmas Mumming in Newfoundland: Essays in Anthropology, Folklore, and History, eds. H. Halpert and G. M. Story (Canada: Univ. of Toronto Press, 1969), p. 38.

5. James C. Faris, "Mummering in an Outport Fishing Settlement: Description and Suggestions on the Cognitive Complex," in Christmas Mumming in Newfoundland, p. 131.

6. Ibid., p. 141.

7. Ibid.

8. Herbert Halpert, "A Typology of Mumming," in Christmas Mumming in Newfoundland, pp. 44-45. Also Shmuel Ben-Dor, "The 'Naluyuks' of Northern Labrador," in Christmas Mumming in Newfoundland.

9. George M. Story, "Newfoundland: Fisherman, Hunters, Planters and Merchants," in Christmas Mumming in Newfoundland, pp. 27-28.

10. Victor Turner, "Symbolic Studies," in Annual Review of Anthropology, v. 4, eds. B. J. Siegel, A. R. Beals, and S. A. Tylor (Calif: Annual Reviews Inc., 1977), pp. 145-162.

11. Herbert Halpert and G. M. Story, Christmas Mumming in Newfoundland, 1969.

12. For a more descriptive account of mummers attacks and the subsequent statutory ban on mummering in Newfoundland in 1861, see G. M. Story, "Newfoundland: Fishermen, Hunters, Planters and Merchants" in Christmas Mumming in Newfoundland, 1969, pp. 26-30.

13. James C. Faris, Cat Harbour: A Newfoundland Fishing Settlement (St. John's, Newfoundland: The Institute of Social and Economic Research, Memorial University, 1972). Melvin Firestone, Brothers and Rivals: Patrilocality in Savage Cove (St. John's, Newfoundland: ISER, Memorial Univ., 1967).

14. C. Grant Head, Eighteenth Century Newfoundland (N.Y.: Carleton Library Books, 1976). R. Matthews, "There's No Better Place Than Here": Social Change in Three Newfoundland Com3 unities (Canada: Peter Martin, Ltd., 1976).

15. Ottar Brox, Newfoundland Fishermen in the Age of Industry: A Study of Economic Dualism (St. John's, Nfld.: ISER, Memorial Univ., 1972).

16. James C. Faris, Cat Harbour (St. John's, Nfld.: ISER, 1972), see especially chapter

17. Thomas Necec, "I Fish with my Brother," in North Atlantic Fishermen, eds. Raoul Andersen and Cato Wadel (St. John's, Nfld: ISER, Memorial Univ., 1972)

18. James C. Faris, Cat Harbour, op. cit., p. 67, ff.

19. Raoul Andersen and C. Wadel, "Comparative Problems in Fishing Adaptations", in North Atlantic Fishermen.

20. James C. Faris, "Mumming in an Outport Fishing Settlement: A Description and Suggestions on the Cognitive Complex," in Christmas Mumming in Newfoundland, p. 138.

21. H. Halpert and G. M. Story (eds.), Christmas Mumming in Newfoundland: Essays in Anthropology, Folklore and History (Canada: Univ. of Toronto Press), 1969.

22. Ibid., chap. 4, 7 and 8.

23. Ibid., chap. 4 and 6.

24. Gerald Sider, "Christmas Mumming and the New Year in Outport Newfoundland," Past and Present, No. 71, May 1976, pp. 102-125.

25. Melvin Firestone, "Mummers and Strangers in Northern Newfoundland," in Christmas Mumming, p. 73.

26. J. C. Faris, "Mumming in an Outport Fishing Settlement: A Description and Suggestions on the Cognitive Complex," in Christmas Mumming, p. 134.

27. Ibid., p. 144.

28. Clifford Geertz, "Deep Play: Notes on the Balinese Cockfight," in C. Geertz, The Interpretation of Cultures, op. cit., p. 448.

29. Ibid., p. 468.

30. J. C. Faris, Cat Harbour, op. cit., p. 161.

CHAPTER SEVEN

"Towards Religion as Semiopraxis: A Critique on the Symbolism

of Clifford Geertz,"

Fritz Holscher
University of South Africa

Abstract

The main argument of this articule is that Geertz's symbolism tends to be objectivistic and thus leads to an alienated view of man. His attempt to revise functionalism
leads to a typical Cartesian problem. However, the merits of his work can be illustrated by creating a dialogue between Geertz, Peter Berger and John O'Malley. The
result then is that man is typified as homo dialogicus, and meaning as human enterprise is taken from its objective pedestal and put into the dialectical context of
human praxis. Religion is therefore regarded as semiopraxis and not as a set of
symbols.

"Meaning as human experience is that which constitutes the sine qua non of culture, and so likewise with religion."[1]

In this quotation John Morgan emphasizes the importance of the concept "meaning" in the study of man, thereby associating himself with Susanne Langer who maintains that "meaning" is one of the crucial philosophical concepts of our age. It was not without reason that Geertz in 1957 commented on the new approach to the study of religion introduced by the view that man is a "symbolizing, concept-ualizing, meaning-seeking animal."[2] In the argument with which we are concerned the process of the investing meaning or, as Morgan expresses it, "meaning as experience," is accentuated. Meaning is thus not seen as a certain amount of pre-fabricated cultural contents to be learned or assimilated by man. Meaning occupies a central position in the nature of man and in his relationship with the world. For this reason John O'Malley type casts man as homo signifier and goes on to say "Man signs himself into his world, which takes shape as a world for him in his signing there his signature — himself."[3]

In spite of their common emphasis on meaning, on first reading it seems as if a contradiction exists in the views of Geertz and O'Malley in Geertz's accentuation of "meaning-seeking" as opposed to O'Malley's assertion "man signs himself . . . " The paradox indicated by these apprently contradictory viewpoints is the subject for discussion in the argument which follows. In the dialogue between Geertz, O'Malley and Berger and Luckmann, there is a swing away from symbolism towards praxis as context for religion. That the contribution of symbolism is by no means underrated is indicated by the concept of semiopraxis. The constitution of meaning and it's relationship with the existential position of man is thus of particular interest. O'Malley neatly delineates the dialectic of the process of constitution of meaning in his comment — "Meaning is the making of man."[4]

At the same time O'Malley defines the context in which the meaning of meaning must be sought, namely human behaviour, experience or praxis. This gives rise to the choice of the term semiopraxis, where semio refers to meaning and praxis to human experience or behaviour.

In our argument special attention is paid to Geertz's definition of religion and his attempt to revise the functionalistic model. Geertz's work is critically evaluated and further expanded by relating it to the work of John O'Malley, Peter Berger and Thomas Luckmann.

I. The Symbolism of Clifford Geertz: 'New wine in old wineskins'.

Like many other thinkers of his day, Geertz was impressed by the numerous shortcomings of the functionalistic model, especially in explaining social change.[5] He comments that functionalism emphasizes stability and equilibrium, and is ultimately prejudiced in favour of "well-integrated societies in a stable equilibrium and a tendency to emphasize the functional aspects of a people's social usage and customs rather than their dysfunctional implications."[6]

Geertz attributes the apparent inability on the part of functional theory to find a satisfactory explanation for change to the deterministic nature of functionalistic theory which quite rightly differentiates between cultural and social systems of behaviour but then either ignores one of the systems, or reduces one system to the mirror image of the other. Geertz tries to approach the problem of change, or the historical dimension as he calls it, by revising the functionalistic model. He maintains that cultural and social systems are not mere reflections of each other but in fact independent and interdependent variables.[7] He aligns himself with Talcott Parsons' discussion of the three systems of behaviour, namely the social, cultural and personality systems, and goes on to refer to the distinction made by Sorokin between "logico-meaningful integration" (culture) and "casual functional integration" (social structure).[8]

Geertz hereby propounds a dualistic model where the two elements are related to each other but not deducible from each other. According to this model, change would be the result of an incongruence between the two systems, and the resultant strain gives rise to adjustment and change in one or both of the systems. This dynamic functionalistic approach is common to theoreticians like Talcott Parsons, Merton, Walter Buckley and others. A common characteristic of various theories adhering to this approach is the Cartesian problem where two categories which logically exclude each other are eclectically combined to form the basis of the theory. Although Geertz does not pay explicit attention to the view of man or a philosophic-anthropological model implied by this dualistic theory, the consequences are nevertheless clear: a view of man with Descartes' theoretical dilemma of a body and soul which are logically and substantially mutually exclusive, but yet both part of man. Like the figure of King Nebuchadnezzar's dream, Geertz's man stands on feet of "iron and clay!" The merits of Geertz's work lie in his attempt to evade determinism by concentrating on the tension between culture and society and on the important part played by meaning in the articulation of culture and society. I refer to his "attempt," because Geertz's definition of religion does not always reflect the caution used in propounding other articles. He defines religion as "A system of symbols which acts to establish powerful, pervasive and long-lasting moods and motivations in men by formulating conceptions of a general order of existence and clothing these conceptions with such an aura of factuality that the moods and motivations seem uniquely realistic."[9] It is strange that Geertz could produce such a definition almost a decade after his attempt to revise functionalism, because in explaining this definition Geertz once again comes up with a definite form of determinism. Religion as a system of symbols is seen as "extrinsic sources of information"[10] which act like genes in an organism to provide a blueprint for human behaviour: " . . . (like genes) culture patterns provide such programs for the institution of the psychological and social processes which shape public behaviour."[11] Culture thus has a particularly dynamic function in society, to the extent that it seems almost to have a self evident power or ability to act. The dynamic nature of culture is also illustrated in Geertz's comment — "Culture patterns have an intrinsic double aspect: they give meaning, i.e. objective conceptual form, to social and psychological reality both by shaping themselves to it and by shaping it to themselves."[12]

Although Geertz tries to preserve the dynamics of his functionalistic theory by the application of an apparently latent form of dialectics in this argument, it is nevertheless not altogether clear how culture acts, or adapts itself. It seems as if Geertz consistently emphasizes a system of symbols external to man and capable of independent action as the initiating factor in religious behaviour. The logical development of such an argument is that human behaviour becomes a reflection of a culture or a religious system of symbols, precisely the conclusion that Geertz wanted to avoid, as I have indicated above. When one system supercedes the other in exercising influence over it, dualism is resolved and Geertz's model can, strictly speaking, be reduced to a form of idealism similar to that found in Max Weber's thesis on the Protestant ethics and the spirit of capitalism. In this thesis Weber demonstrates how human behaviour is determined by a set of values. The philosophic anthrpological consequences of this line of thought are obvious as Marx pointed out about Hegel's man, Geertz's man is standing on his head!

It thus becomes clear why Geertz speaks of man as a "meaning-seeking animal." Man seeks meaning because he is looking for a haven. His life must become significant or meaningful by virtue of the internalization of meanings from outside himself. In this respect, Geertz again aligns himself with Talcott Parsons who indicates that through the process of internalization values, norms and meaning, are so imprinted in man's consciousness that he inevitably has a need to conform to these; human behaviour thereby becomes a reflection, or mirror image of internalized culture. Geertz describes this formative process initiated by the system of symbols as follows:

"They (symbols) both express the world's climate and shape it. They shape it by inducing in the worshipper a certain distinctive set of dispositions which lend a chronic character to the flow of his activity and the quality of his experience."[13] In summary: An ideal-typical construction of Geertz's dynamic functional symbolism would amount to two systems, a cultural and a social system which articulate as independent yet interdependent variables. Geertz attempts to solve the Cartesian problem of dualism by postulating a system of symbols which serves as a blueprint for human behaviour, a system which is simultaneously a model <u>for</u> and a model <u>of</u> social and psychological reality.[14] This culture or system of symbols seems to be self evident, adjusting and changing itself, and serving as motivational dispositions in and for human behaviour.

Consequently, man becomes a product of an external, objective system on which he is dependent:

"Man depends on symbols and symbol systems with a dependence so great as to be decisive for his creatural viability, and his sensitivity to even the remotest indication that they may prove unable to cope with one or another aspect of experience raises within him the gravest sort of anxiety."[15]

Geertz illustrates such an anxiety experience in his description of the confusion of norms which arose at the Javanese funeral.[16]

Durkheim's concept of anomie also denotes this type of insecurity about the norms determining behaviour in a particular situation. By indicating the high suicide rate in anomic situations, Durkheim unambiguously spells out the consequences of social and personal anxiety. Unavoidable questions arise — why does anomie inevitably lead to anxiety and suicide? Is man really so utterly dependent on a system of symbols? Why do some people have exactly the opposite experience in an anomic situation? Why do some people deliberately try to create or perpetuate an anomic situation?

These questions bring us face to face with an important problem in Geertz's work, that of alienation. Geertz's theoretical framework clearly explains the fear of anomie, in that man is socialized towards a dependence of a given external culture. This socialization results in an emotional trauma when a confusion of norms occurs, as Geertz indicated in his description of the Javanese funeral. This trauma is the result of a feeling of powerlessness on the part of man who feels incapable of constituting any other norms for action. Man is alienated as a result of his total dependence on a system of symbols. Jean Paul Satre called this form of alienation "bad faith," and it can also be related to M. Seeman's concept of "powerlessness." Geertz's solution for anomic terror lies in the ability of the system of symbols to adapt itself to the changed situation. According to Sartre's definition, Geertz's man remains in a state of "bad faith," his alienation the inevitable result of the process of socialization which involves him in the internalization of a certain culture in order for him to 'become human.'

This process of socialization, where man is required to identify with an objectified culture or meaning structure to the extent of becoming a mirror image of it, leads to another form of alienation delineated by Marx in his concept of "thinification' (verdinglinchung). Georg Lukacs elaborated on this concept, calling it reification. Marx and Lukacs would thus level the criticism at Geertz that his theory leads to a reified view of man in society. According to Geertz, this situation is functional for the maintenance of the system, and because man is socialized to conform, he would experience a sense of security in such an eunomic situation.[17] However, the underlying fear of anomic terror would remain. A further criticism of Geertz's theory implied by the Marx model would be the fact that the initiative for cultural change lies with man and not within the ability of the system of symbols to adapt itself. Marx introduced the concept of conscientization to emphasize that man can be made conscious of the fact that he himself produces the culture, and that the initiative for reporduction lies with him. Thus, when man becomes aware of his abilities, he would experience a sense of security in such an eunomic situation.

However, the underlying fear of anomic terror would remain. A further criticism of Geertz's theory implied by the Marx model would be the fact that the initiative for cultural change lies with man and not within the ability of the system of symbols to adapt itself. Marx introduced the concept of conscientization to emphasize that man can be made conscious of the fact that he himself produces the culture, and that the initiative for reproduction or adaptation lies with him. Thus, when man becomes aware of his abilities he can save himself from the anomic terror by becoming actively involved in the changing of his culture. In the light of this it is understandable that Marx could adopt Feuerbach's theory that religion is merely the projection of man's own consciousness. If we follow Marx's solution to its logical conclusion, we are brought to a point where man experiences an 'eunomic terror,' where religion and culture are a threat to human freedom and in fact bring about what Marx calls a false consciousness. Geertz thus has every right to accuse Marx of presenting an alienated picture of man, devoid of religion or 'culture.' This ideal-typical Marxian argument does not solve the problem, but leaves us with a Geertz-Marx deadlock!

The burning questions remain unanswered — what is the relationship between man and culture? How does change take place? What in the nature of symbols and meaning systems brings about changes? These questions bring us back to a valuable suggestion by John Morgan in his article "Religion and Culture as meaning systems." In this article Morgan adds new perspective to the work of Geertz by means of a Geertz-Tillich dialogue, and finds 'meaning' to be the link or mediating factor between Geertz and Tillich. Of further importance is the alternative context for meaning suggested by Morgan in his discussion of "meaning as human experience." In this argument Morgan takes meaning from its objective pedestal and palces it in the context where it belongs, namely praxis. The following discussion is based on Morgan's suggestion, but, instead of Tillich, John O'Malley, Peter Berger and Thomas Luckmann, join in the dialogue on religion as semiopraxis.

In this discussion we are concerned with two main problem areas in the work of Geertz — firstly, the Cartesian dualism of his argument, and, secondly, the fact that his 'objectivistic symbolism' apparently leads to a view of an alienated man, reified in a state of false consciousness and bad faith. These two problem areas will serve as points of reference in the presentation of an alternative model.

I will deal with the problem of dualism by introducing the concept dialectic or dialogue. The significance of this concept for the philosophic-anthropological model which underlies my argument is the classification of man as homo dialogicus. With homo dialogicus as point of departure we search for an alternative to the functionalistic model. From this alternative theoretical framework we will attempt to throw new light on the Geertz-Marx deadlock and thus also the problem of alienation.

II. Homo dialogicus

The assigning of a new genus and species classification to man is not new. Max Scheler calls man homo viator, Dahrendorf calls him homo sociologicus, O'Malley classifies him as homo signifier, Durkheim via Zijderveld calls man homo duplex et.[18] For the purpose of this argument man is classified as homo dialogicus. The choice of this particular classification does not necessarily imply a rejection of the other names, but is made for the purposes of a specific argument.

Geertz's dualistic point of view as indicated above could possibly lead to the anthropological point of departure called homo duplex by Zijderveld. The problems arising from such a dualism have already been indicated. This dualism can be solved by a monism, which Geertz seems to prefer, or by the application of a dialectic. By classifying man as homo dialogicus we emphasize his sociality without pleading in favour of a sociologism or Dahrendorf's homo sociologicus. Man is a relating being, constantly in relationship with everything and everyone he encounters, even with himself. The inevitability of this dialogic relationship is not based only on the fact that man is continually confronted with the transcendent (the Absolute), material and social objects; man's dialogic nature or sociality is a result of his capacity for self consciousness or, as Helmuth Plessner calls it, his eccentricity. As a result of his eccentricity man cannot be conditioned like an animal, and his behaviour can also not be determined instinctively because he is homo dialogicus. He is constantly in dialogue with his "Umwelt" which he moulds by this means into a life-world.

As early as 500 BC Heraclitus formulated the basic problem underlying the concept dialects, and with certain adaptations this concept figures in the work of the Sophists, Socrates and Plato, but it is in the work of Hegel and Marx in particular that the concept is actualized for modern day thought. This is neither the time nor the place to begin a discussion on the dialectics of Marx and Hegel, but suffice it to say that the interpretation and application of the concept dialectics for the purposes of this argument are not in line with the interpretation made by some scholars of Marx and Hegel. The popular conception of dialectics is historistic[19] in nature and concentrates on the sequence of three dialectical steps, namely thesis, antithesis, and synthesis, which in its turn changes into a thesis to sets the whole process in motion once again. In contrast to this process, in this article the concept involves a reflexive dialectics where tension, difference or opposition are constantly maintained. This state does not imply a functionalistic equilibrium aimed at the maintenance of the status quo, but rather a dialogic situation where dialogue serves as the dynamic basis for the constitution of a life-world. This life-world is by no means static, but is continually being reconstituted by the meaning attached to it by man. As O'Malley puts it, man is involved in the constant rewriting of his own history.[20]

We are now faced with the question of how this dialogue takes place. What is the nature and content of the dialogue? The dialogic nature of man's existence can be further explained by the philosophic anthropological model of Peter Berger and Thomas Luckmann.

III. A Dialectical model of man

Although the most important concepts for this model have been taken from the work of Berger and Luckmann, a reinterpretation has been made to fit the context relevant to this discussion.

Like many other biologists and philosophical anthropologists (including Adolf Portman, Arnold Gehlen, Max Scheler, Plessner amongst others), Berger starts out from the point of view that man, unlike animals, is born incomplete. There is also no man-world as there is a lion-world or dog-world. "Man's world is imperfectly programmed by his own constitution. It is an open world."[21]

By means of his dialogue with his Umwelt man transforms it into a life-world for himself. The dialectic that characterizes his existence bears with it an inbuilt instability in man, and because there is no given relationship between man and his world, man himself has constantly to establish the relationship. This insecurity results in man being out of step with himself and with the world:

"Human existence is an ongoing 'balancing act' between man and his body, man and his world."[22]

The result of this 'balancing act' is culture, defined by Berger as "the totality of man's products."[23] Berger goes on to indicate that society is in actual fact an element of culture, specifically, of non-material culture. It would appear that Berger is exposing himself to Geertz's criticism that culture and society cannot be subordinated to each other. If this is the case, then Berger would, in fact, be repudiating his own argument, because, in terms of the basic assumptions of Berger's argument, culture and society form a dialectical unity. Of more importance is that the culture-society discourse becomes a chicken-or-the-egg problem when homo dialogicus is used as theoretical point of departure. The implications are far-reaching; with homo dialogicus as point of departure, the functionalistic model is not only revised, but replaced with a radically different alternative model. This model is based on and deduced from the phenomenon being investigated, namely human praxis, unlike the functionalistic model which is deduced from the biological sciences "where the term function is understood to refer to the vital organic processes considered in the respects in which they contribute to the maintenance of the organism."[24] The untenableness of any attempt to describe and analyse man according to a system alien to man has already been pointed out. The concept "function" can nevertheless be of value for the dialogic model, with the proviso that the concept is defined in terms of the requirements of the dialectical model.

Berger further explains his dialectical model by indicating that the dialogue or relationship of man with his <u>Umwelt</u> develops through the articulation of three existential moments namely externalization, internalization and objectivation. I have already explained that, in the light of the dialectical viewpoint of this particular argument, the different moments must be seen simultaneously and not, as favoured by the historistic dialecticians, as consecutive steps. The three moments collectively and simultaneously make up the dialogue. Berger summarizes the three moments as follows:

"Externalization is the ongoing outpouring of human being into the world, both in the physical and the mental activity of men. Objectivation is the attainment by the products of this activity (again both physical and mental) of a reality that confronts its original producers as a facticity external to and other than themselves. Internalization is the reappropriation by men of this same reality, transforming it once again from structures of the objective world into structures of the subjective consciousness."[25]

Man does not pour himself out into a vacuum, in his encounter with his Umwelt he is constantly confronted with objects with which he may enter into idalogue or 'ex-istential'[26] opportunities. By saying that the world is open, Berger does not imply a tabula rasa offering man unlimited scope for projection. The process of objectivation subjects man to limiting factors[27] within the objective world. At this point we can join Martin Buber, Berkhof and even William James who describe man's 'partners' in dialogue as the transcendent, (the Absolute) the social or fellow man, and the material.

These dimensions of man's Umwelt must also be seen in a dialectical unity, as is emphasized by Buber:

"Neither the world of things, nor his fellow-man and community, nor true mystery which points beyond these, and also himself, can be dismissed from a man's situation."[28]

Objectivation is the embodiment of man in an object outside himself. Here we again join Geertz. Religious symbols can thus be seen as the embodiment of man's relationship or dialogue with the transcendent, which includes man's fellow-man and his material world. Symbols are in actual fact not objects alien to man, but objectified human behaviour. A prerequisite for objectivation is not only externalization (and, of course, vice versa), but also internalization. By means of internalization man becomes conscious of objectified reality, and of himself as objectified reality in that he makes this objectified reality part of his consciousness. If the process were to stop at this point, as is the case in Geertz's model discussed above, we would here be theoretically dealing with an existential short circuit or undialogical consciousness[29] indicating a state of alienation. This state of alienation can be averted by man realizing his nature through continuing dialogue with himself and his Umwelt.

The dialogic nature of man's existence implies a perpetuation of a state of marginality.[30] Homo dialogicus can never really 'come home' or be totally absorbed in a prefabricated culture. He can never become the mirror image of a set of expectations as is postulated by Alant: "Our relationships with our fellow men and 'the world' have to be revised continually as we always meet each other as changing persons in new situations."[31] To meet each other as changing persons in new situations is possible because of the existential dialogue through which man confronts everything around him, this existential dialogue, however, does not merely refer to praxis, but to semiopraxis, because dialectical praxis is in fact constitutive of meaning. When meaning becomes such an integral part of dialogue it can not merely be regarded as symbolic interaction.

Meaning is much more comprehensive than symbols, symbolizing is but one aspect of the constitution of meaning. Against this background religion is referred to as semiopraxis. After having discussed the dialectic nature of praxis, the argument is taken a step further through the exploration of the concepts of meaning via the work of John O'Malley.

IV. "Meaning is the Making of Man"

Berger's dialectical model should provide us with a more comprehensive grasp of the implications of this quotation. Man tries to arrive at a state of completion in and through a world of meaning. O'Malley describes the importance of man's encounter with his Umwelt as follows: "For meaning is the dialectic of encounter through which it becomes in fact man's mediation of himself."[32] Meaning is thus the dynamic or dialectical substance or matrix of the encounter between man and his Umwelt. In the light of this, O'Malley's concept of the mediating function of meaning becomes clearer. As a result of the mediating function of meaning it is undialectical to speak of meaning that is only internalized or only externalized. O'Malley elaborates: "Uttering (externalization) and hearkening (internalization) together comprise meaning. They are twin indissociable aspects of its single integral act that constitutes[33] the meant as meaningful for man" (Italics and brackets mine).

According to this argument it would be equally undialectical to speak of objectified meaning. To provide for this O'Malley distinguishes between objectivization and objectification, where objectivization refers to a moment in the dialectical process and objectification to undialectical reification.[34] Culture and religion as such an objective system of symbols would indicate reification in terms of a dialectical model. Although the concepts of mediation does not figure explicitly in Geertz's work, a few valuable clues, such as his reference to "symbols as vehicles for conception,"[35] indicate a certain sensitivity to the process. A problem in Geertz's theory is the fact that these symbols become "translucent" in man's relationship with himself, his God, his fellow man and the world. The worshipper's religious world becomes such a cordon of translucent symbols or objectified meaning structures that it becomes impossible for him to perceive his fellow man or his God. True dialogue or encounter can only take place when meaning becomes transparent. Translucent or reified meaning causes man to lose contact with his 'partner' and become involved in a pseudo encounter. True encounter is described by O'Malley as follows:

"Encounter, then, as existential dialogue, is not instant deliverance of self and other. It is a mutual creation through reciprocal constitution of each other. It is mediated through genuine communication in which together we actualize our meaningfulness for and with each other. Thus we question others as we question ourselves . . . about ourselves and each other."[36] (italics mine) By ascribing a mediating function to meaning, another possible misunderstanding in Gertz's work is resolved. When he compares symbols to genetic material, the logical conclusion is that human behaviour becomes the expression of culture. Mediation in this context would imply that human behaviour fulfills a mediating function for culture. In terms of the dialectical model both behaviour (praxis) and meaning fulfill a mediating function by virtue of the dialogic nature of the encounter or semiopraxis.

The dialectical model in terms of which religion is described as semiopraxis can be schematically presented as follows:

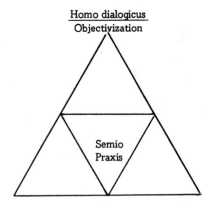

Homo dialogicus
Objectivization

Semio
Praxis

Externalization   Internalization

V. Alienation as 'undialectical consciousness'

Lack of space prohibits a systematic discussion of the different forms of alienation. The few cursory comments above, supplemented by the following suggestions, must suffice. Berger formulates alienation as "undialectical consciousness"[37] and Beerling formulates it as "undialectical stagnation".[38] This implies that the dialectics that characterize homo dialogicus' existence can 'stagnate' at any one of the three existential moments and produce the following forms of alienation. As far as objectivation is concerned, reification as a form of alienation has already been mentioned. The implications of this for e.g. the stereotyping of people are obvious. As far as internalization is concerned, reference has been made to Sartre's concept of bad faith and Seeman's concept of powerlessness. When the dialectic stagnates at externalization, 'fantasy' or social autism arises. Although reference has been made to the work of other authors in this connection, all indicators of the empirical appearance of alienation could not be indiscriminately applied in the case of the above mentioned typology. Further empirical investigation is necessary to devise a scale for alienation with reference to this typology.

VI. Empirical Relevance and Conclusions

It is doubtless an ambitious undertaking to find an alternative to functionalism which is as easily empirically enforceable. The challenge grows in stature in the light of the amount of research which has sprung from the marriage of functionalistic theory and positivistic methodology. The first test of good social theory does not in fact lie in its capacity for operationalization as far as empirical research is concerned, but rather in the degree of understanding which it brings for and of man and his life-world. This does not, however, release the scientist from the requirements of operationalization as far as empirical research is concerned. The value of the discussion between Geertz, Berger and O'Malley lies in the fact that it postulates an alternative to functionalism, and does not merely offer a revision of functionalism as Geertz initially suggested. The dialectical theory is particularly valuable in that it offers questions and answers which are beyond the scope of functionalism. Special attention in the discussion was paid to Geertz's criticism that functionalism fails to offer a satisfactory explanation for change, and thus the aspect of change was emphasized while other aspects were merely mentioned in passing. The dialectical model is of special advantage in the study of phenomena like new religious movements of which the Charismatic or Neo-Pentecostal movement is but one example. After almost two decades this movement seems to have a fairly close relationship with the churches of their historical origin. This relationship is maintained in spite of the movement's reaction against and criticism of these churches, although the historical churches often seem to be very anti-Charismatic. Another very interesting characteristic of the movement is its ecumenical nature. Where the historical churches seem to be a-ecumentical or even separatistic, the Charismatics constantly encourage ecumenical contact. This ecumenical contact does not seem to initiate the formation of a new church or denomination, although there is evidence of sectarian splits which have occurred.

The following questions seem to have some relevance for further empirical research on the basis of the proposed dialectical model. Is the ecumenical nature of the movement a manifestation of dialogue? Is the reaction against the historical churches an attempt to avoid a state of alienation which could be the result of separatism in Christianity? What are the demands of dialogue both for the historical churches and for the Charismatic movement? Can the Charismatic movement avoid moving from one form of alienation to another? To what extent do religious symbols and meaning (e.g. speaking in tongues and other charismatic gifts) remain transparent? These are only a few questions on a macro sociological level.

The dialectical model would also serve as framework for study on a micro level, giving rise to the following sort of questions: What is the nature of group cohesion in the Charismatic small group? What is the nature of the socialization process and that of the process of proselitizing? How does the individual react to anomic or eunomic situations? What is the nature of leadership? What is the role of the charismatic leader? What is the nature of relationships within the group or movement as well as outside the group or movement? What are the implications of the religious experience for more secular relationships involving, for example, differences in race, language and social class?

Although most of these questions could also be studied within a functionalistic frame of reference, the lines of argument and the conclusions would certainly differ in many instances. The nature and scope of dialogue, or the manifest absence of dialogue (alienation) seem to be an important indicator for the nature of the cohabitation of people, especially in societies of a plural nature, where change is continually taking place as a result of cultural contact. And this seems to be one of the major social scientific challenges of our day!

NOTES

1. Morgan, John: "Religion and culture as meaning systems: a dialogue between Geertz and Tillich." The Journal of Religion (Vol. 57 no. 4 October 1979) p. 365.

2. As quoted by Morgan op. cit. p. 363.

3. O'Malley, John B: "The sociology of meaning" (London: Human context Books n.d.) p. 115.

4. O'Malley op. cit. p. 110.

5. Geertz, Clifford: "Ritual and Social change: an Javanese example" (in Lessa, W.A. & Vogt, E.Z. eds. "Reader in Comparative religion" New York: Harper & Row 1965) p. 547-559.

6. Ibid. p. 548.

7. Ibid. p. 548.

8. Ibid. p. 549.

9. Geertz, Clifford "Religion as Cultural System" in Reader in Comparitive religion: (Lessa, W. A. & Vogt E. Z. ed. New York: Harper & Row 1965) p. 206.

10. Ibid. p. 206

11. Ibid. p. 207.

12. Ibid. p. 207.

14. Ibid. p. 209.

15. Ibid. p. 109.

16. Ibid. p. 547.

17. Leo Srole distinguishes between an anomic and an eunomic situation where eunomy refers to a situation where the norms are clearly defined and anomie,

of course, implies just the opposite. Srole, L. in Finifter Ada, W. (ed) "Alienation and the Social System": New York; John Wiley & Sons Inc., 1972) p. 61.

18. Also see Morgan, John H.: "Religious myth and symbol". in (Philosophy today; Vol. 18 Sprin 1974) p. 82.

19 For a discussion of historism in this regard, see Karl R. Popper "The Open Societies and its enemies" (London: Routledge & Kegan Paul 1973) Vol. 2.

20 O'Malley op. cit. p. 2.

21. Berger, Peter L. "The Sacred Canopy" (New York: Anchor Books 1969) p. 5.

22. Ibid. p. 5-6.

23. Ibid. p. 6.

24. Merton, Robert K.: "Social theory and Social structure" (London: Collier Macmillan, 1957) p. 21.

25. Berger op. cit. p. 4.

26. "Ex-istential, as it is used here, literary refers to the original Latin where "ex" and "sisto" means to "step outside."

27. Maritz, F. A. in Meyer, A.M.T. et al. "Die fenomenologie" (Pretoria-Kaapstad, Academica 1967) makes the important distinction between 'limiting' and 'determining' factors.

28. Buber, Martin "Between man and man" (London: Fontana Library 1961) p. 218.

29. Berger op. cit. p. 85 refers to undialectical consciousness in this regard.

30. Also see Karl Jasper's Concept "Grenzsituation" in this respect as well as Martin Heidegger.

31. Alant, C. J. "Migrant labour and the church: Has the church got any options?" (Pretoria: University of South Africa 1976) p. 4.

32. O'Malley op. cit. p. 111.

33. Ibid. p. 117.

34. Ibid. p. 122.

35. Geertz "Religion as a cultural system" p. 206.

36. O'Malley op. cit. p. 121.

37. Berger op. cit. p. 85.

38. Beerling, R. F. "Wijsgerig sociologiesche verkeningen" (Van Loghum Statarus Arnheim, W. de Haan Zeist 1964) p. 103-110.

CHAPTER EIGHT

"Javanese Ritual and Geertz's Interpretation: A Rebuttal,"*

James O. Buswell III
Wheaton College

*This paper was presented at the 76th Annual Meeting of the
American Anthropological Association, Houston, Texas, December 2, 1977.

Abstract

In his still widely reprinted essay, "Ritual and Social Change," Geertz critiques

functionalist claims of the stabilizing influence of religion by describing a funeral

ritual as "tearing the society apart rather than integrating it." His own evidence

suggests, instead, that political changes precipitated the conflict, and that the

religious ritual would have provided its traditional function but for the political

disruption. Implications are drawn for critics of "static functionalism."

The essay, "Ritual and Social Change: A Javanese Example," by Clifford Geertz, originally published in the Anthropologist twenty years ago (Geertz 1957), has achieved somewhat the status of a classic. Reprinted again and again in anthologies (e.g., Lessa and Vogt, eds., 1958, 1965, and 1972; Schneider, ed., 1964; Demerath and Peterson, eds., 1967), including Geertz's own volume of selected essays (Geertz 1973), and widely circulated as a Bobbs-Merrill reprint (A-78), its theoretical contribution is also cited in appropriate contexts by current authors (e.g., Yinger, 1970, pp. 90, 152; Malefijt, 1974, p. 212; Keesing, 1974, p. 79.)

The essay describes in some detail a dramatic case of a Javanese funeral and Slametan ritual which was seriously disrupted and almost failed completely before emergency procedural adjustments did allow the ritual to be completed amidst social tension, emotional outbursts, and grumbling.

Geertz used this case not only as a critique of what he claimed was the functionalists' inability to deal with social change in general, but also as a critique of their view of the role of religion in society in particular.

First he assigned the funeral ritual itself to the category of "religion" and thus to "culture" as an example of Sorokin's "logico-meaningful integration;" and the social interaction involved he assigned to "social structure" illustrating Sorokin's "causal-functional integration."

"It is the thesis of this paper," Geertz wrote, "that one of the major reasons for the inability of functional theory to cope with change lies in its failure to treat sociological and cultural processes on equal terms" (p. 33). As far as the emphasis upon the analytical distinction between change in cultural complexes and change in the social structure is concerned, the contribution is not unsound, but merely over-simplified. In order to demonstrate this, however, Geertz describes functionalists' stress upon "the harmonizing, integrating, and psychologically supportive aspects of religious patterns" (p. 32), claiming that his "more dynamic functionalist approach" applied to the "particular case of a ritual which failed to function properly" will have a greater utility in accounting for the ritual failure analyzing "more explicitly the cause of the trouble." "It will further be argued," he wrote, "that such an approach is able to avoid the simplistic view of the functional role of religion in society which sees that role merely as structure-conserving . . . " (p. 34). A re-examination of this focus upon religion in the proving of his thesis is long overdue.

In the first place the "simplistic view of the functional role of religion in society which sees that role merely as structure-conserving" is a "straw man," as is the widely-used characterization of functionalism as "this static, ahistorical approach," or "static functionalism," or the "static view of social structure," all used by Geertz in this essay. Since Geertz refers specifically to Radcliffe-Brown, and more particularly to Malinowski in his critique, I shall do the same in an attempt to indicate perhaps a more realistic perspective on the dynamic functionalism that I believe they had in mind.

As soon as Radcliffe-Brown and Malinowski got off their respective islands and back into the "real world," so to speak, their limited functionalism changed considerably. Regarding Radcliffe-Brown's view of the role of religious ritual in society, we may refer to his 1939 paper on "Taboo." For a "theory of ritual first worked out in 1908" (1952:152), it proves at least awareness of functions of religion never attributed to functionalists by their critics. Here, following discussion of the "structure-conserving" function of rites used to restore and retain confidence in uncertainty and danger, he says,

> I think that for certain rites it would be easy to maintain with equal plausibility an exact contrary theory, namely, that if it were not for the existence of the rite and the beliefs associated with it, the individual would feel no anxiety, and that the psychological effect of the rite is to create in him a sense of insecurity or danger . . .

> Thus, while one anthropological theory is that magic and religion give men confidence, comfort and a sense of security, . . . it could equally well be argued that they give men fears and anxieties from which they would otherwise be free . . . (1952:148-149).

Malinowski, in 1938, referring to a sentiment he had expressed as early as 1929, for example, wrote that,

> . . . we must face the new, more complex and more difficult task which history has set before us, the task that is of building new methods and new principles of research . . . and take up the "new branch of anthropology . . . the anthropology of the changing native." (Malinowski 1938:xii).

Furthermore, he was well aware at that time that,

> A society obviously cannot be "well integrated" and "undergoing a revolution" at one and the same time! A glance at the role of European culture agents will show where the concept of a well-integrated whole breaks down. (Ibid. p. xv).

Malinowski also, with his distinguished students at that time, was grappling with the very kinds of confused and conflicting lines of change with which Geertz was dealing:

> Change also generally implies maladjustment, deterioration, social strain, and confusion in legal and moral principles. (Ibid. p. xxv). It is necessary, I think, to make it plain once and for all that to treat the process of acculturation as a static product, in which Europeans and Africans have arrived at a state of temporary integration or of harmonized unity, is unprofitable. (Ibid. p. xxiv).

Then, as for the distinction between the social and and cultural elements within his view of the role of supernatural beliefs in society, Malinowski, writing of witchcraft as a "symptom of economic distress, of social tension, of political or social oppression" and observing that, "In Africa, culture change produces, on the whole, conditions of economic distress, political unrest, and personal conflicts" (1945:97), made the crucial distinctions as follows:

> Now I submit that the common measure between the rational and logical approach to witchcraft and Native belief must be looked for in the sociological context of human malice, competition, and sense of injury, which form the actual framework in social relationships, upon which the supernatural power has always to work. (Ibid. Emphasis mine).

Thus when Malinowski writes that,

> . . . religion counteracts the centrifugal forces of fear, dismay, demoralization, and provides the most powerful means of reintegration of the group's shaken solidarity and of the re-establishment of its morale" (1948: pp. 33-35, quoted by Geertz, p. 48),

he is not excluding the possibility of change or process, nor is he really saying anything more than Geertz himself has claimed for the function of the Slametan ritual when he pointed out that,

> The result of this quiet, undramatic little ritual is twofold: the spirits are appeased and the neighborhood solidarity is strengthened (p. 36).

Geertz also speaks of "a sense of communnity which the slametan clearly reinforces" (Ibid.). And again, "the whole momentum of the Javanese ritual system is supposed to carry one through grief without severe emotional disturbance . . . for the neighborhood group it is said to produce rukun, 'communal harmony' " (p. 40).

In such a context, then, let us briefly review the series of events which transpired on the particular occasion in question in order to determine whether or not the religious ritual was, as Geertz claimed, "the center and source of stress" (p. 48).

There were two politico-religious parties, the Islam-based Masjumi, and the anti-Islamic Permai. The funeral ritual was one of long tradition and marked syncretism which contained certain Islamic elements prominent within it. Whereas the Permai party advocated continuation of rituals without their "Islamic" content, Geertz points out that "because of the long history of syncretism, they are so deeply involved with Islamic customs that a genuinely non-islamic funeral tends to be a practical impossibility" (p. 39).

One element common to all concerned was the traditional necessity to conduct the ritual with dispatch lest the spirit of the deceased remain too long in the vicinity. To delay matters was considered to be extremely dangerous. Both parties also, according to Geertz, were characterized generally by "the easy tolerance of the Javanese for a wide range of religious concepts, so long as the basic ritual patterns —

i.e., slametans — were faithfully supported" (p. 37). This particular burial ritual was common to all members of the community and provided the only ritual known to members of both parties by which the dead should be buried.

The dead boy in this case belonged to a family of the anti-Islamic Permai; but the only practitioners, the Modins, who perform the burial ceremonies, are local leaders of the opposite, Islamic-oriented party. Since political friction was growing with the Permai leaders becoming more overtly anti-Islamic in their efforts for political recognition, the Modins of the opposite party were ordered not to officiate any longer at the funerals of Permai. This caught the local members of the Permai completely off-guard. As Geertz points out, when the Modin, seeing the political symbol in the yard of the deceased, refused to proceed with the funeral of the young boy, the uncle with whom the boy had lived was

> . . . rather upset at all this and evidently surprised, for . . . it had evidently never occurred to him that the anti-Moslem-funeral agitation of the party would ever appear as a concrete problem, or that the Modin would actually refuse to officiate (p. 41).

There was no contradiction in the mind of the local Permai members between their anti-Masjumi political stance and their traditional cultural expectations of the burial ritual.

The uncle appealed to a policeman friend who advised the Modin, "that according to time-honored custom he was supposed to bury everyone with impartiality, never mind whether he happened to agree with their politics" (p. 41).

Meanwhile, the news of the boy's death had been circulated and "the entire neighborhood was already gathering for the ceremony" (p. 42).

Geertz points out that despite the growing alienation socially and politically, the demonstration of territorial unity at a funeral was still felt by both groups to be an unavoidable duty; of all the Javanese rituals, the funeral probably carries the greatest obligation on attendance. Everyone who lives within a certain roughly defined radius of the survivors' home is expected to come to the ceremony; and on this occasion everyone did (p. 42).

In the absence of the Modin, Geertz explains,

. . . it was clear that the ritual was arrested and that no one quite knew what to do next. Tension slowly rose. People nervously watched the sun rise higher and higher in the sky, . . . Mutterings about the sorry state of affairs began to appear: "everything these days is a political problem," an old traditionalistic man of about eighty grumbled to me, "you can't even die any more but what it becomes a political problem" (p. 43).

Because of the danger of delay, a young layman volunteered to initiate some of the necessary preparation of the body so that they could at least get on with the ceremony as best they could. Shortly the Modin arrived on the scene and challenged the Permai leaders to take charge of their own funeral, but " . . . they finally refused, with some chagrin, saying they really did not know how to go about it" (p. 44).

The father and mother then arrived from a distant town. When the young volunteer director of the ceremony put it up to the father as to how he wished the boy to be buried, Geertz reported that,

> The father, somewhat bewildered, said, "Of course, the Islamic way. I don't have much of any religion, but I'm not a Christian, and when it comes to death, the burial should be the Islamic way. Completely Islamic" (p. 45).

The young volunteer apologized to the father. "It was too bad," he said, "about all the tension that was in the air, that political differences had to make so much trouble" (p. 45). The funeral was then completed in routine fashion.

Now in the context of the functionalist view of religion's role, that of maintaining and restoring social cohesion and solidarity, Geertz interprets this case study to prove the contrary. "It seemed," he said, "as if the ritual were tearing the society apart rather than integrating it, were disorganizing personalities rather than healing them." "As a matter of fact," he continued, "it is around religious beliefs and practices . . . that the most seriously disruptive events seem to cluster" (p. 48). And again, with reference to the average townsman, "Amid a radically more complex social environment, he clings noticeably to the symbols which guided him and his parents through life in rural society. And it is this fact," Geertz insisted, "which gave rise to the psychological and social tensions surrounding Paidjan's funeral" (p. 49, emphasis mine).

Yet Geertz is careful to point out that "the symbols which compose the slametan had both religious and political significance, were charged with both sacred and profane import" (p. 49). If that was the case, why did Geertz select the religious ones as the source and cause of the conflict instead of the political ones? It was, after all, the political cleavage which caused the conflict whereas Geertz presented abundant evidence that everyone agreed upon the religious aspects. He even enlarged on this:

There was no argument over whether the slametan pattern was the correct ritual, whether the neighbors were obligated to attend, or whether the supernatural concepts upon which the ritual is based were valid ones. For both [parties] . . . the slametan maintains its force as a genuine sacred symbol; it still provides a meaningful framework for facing death — for most people the only meaningful framework (p. 49).

Thus, it is my contention that the ceremony would have provided all of the cohesive functions expected of it by everybody, had it not been disrupted by political actions.

More surprising even than Geertz' naming religion as the cause of the disruption are his apparently conflicting thoughts regarding the relationships of the religious, the political, and other kinds of change. He said at one point that "This disrupted funeral was in fact but a microcosmic example of the broader conflicts . . . " (p. 35). Yet in his analysis he calimed that "Religion here is somehow the center and source of stress, not merely the reflection of stress elsewhere in the society" (p. 48). Taking his statements charging religion with disruption, one might paraphrase them in terms of the notorious disruption of the educational proceedings at Little Rock, Arkansas, in 1957 when Governor Faubus used armed troops to prevent nine black students from entering Central High School:

It seemed as if the [schools] were tearing the society apart rather than integrating it, were disorganizing personalities rather than healing them.

Or:

> As a matter of fact, it is around the [educational system] that the most seriously disruptive events seem to cluster. [Education] here is somehow the center and source of stress, not merely the reflection of stress elsewhere in the society.

Instead of "The rituals themselves" becoming "matters of political conflict" as Geertz claimed (p. 51), it was, rather, whether or not to provide the rituals which became the matter of political conflict. Instead of "the religious form" going "against the grain of social equilibrium" as Geertz claimed (p. 52), it was a political act which went against the grain.

The slametan case thus does not invalidate Malinowski's claims for integrative religious functions any more than the most "un-Zuni" initiation whippings invalidate Ruth Benedict's claims of an Appollonian pattern for Pueblo culture as has been claimed by some of her critics. Malinowski was fully as much aware of the dynamics of socio-cultural change and political disruption in colonial Africa as Benedict was of Pueblo initiation rites. They both wrote important and valid generalizations for their times, in other-things-being-equal contexts. But, whereas changes in such contexts certainly alter the conditions and applicability of the generalization, they do not invalidate them. In the case at hand the specifications of contextual changes are used to criticize the functionalist generalization as such rather than to qualify it by pointing out limitations of its applicability.

Finally, Geertz's explanation, that it was the persistence of a peasant cultural "religious symbol system" within a changing urban social structure (p. 53), which resulted in the discontinuity between them is over-simplified. Both the religious elements and the political elements are cultural in Geertz's terms, as well as constituting a "social system" to the extent that they each include a "pattern of social interaction itself" (p. 33), peculiar to their own cultural existence, sometimes distinct (as when in political debate); sometimes coinciding (as when attending a funeral slametan), interwoven in different forms of social structure. The culture and and the social structure are, as Geertz rightly emphasizes, "but different abstractions from the same phenomena" (p. 34).

Thus the case study turns out to be not so much a demonstration of the "inherent incongruity and tension between" a conservative religious culture and a more swiftly changing social structure, (p. 33). Rather it is a demonstration of one cultural institution, (religious ritual), more traditional and changing slowly, involving a unified social structure; and another, (political parties), introduced more recently, and changing more radically, but splitting the very same social system into two political factions which remained unified in their ritual expectations.

To preserve all of the importance of the dramatic case, to enhance Geertz's obvious gift for analytical precision as well as to maintain the theoretical significance of the essay, a revision could well disengage it from the vulnerable arguments against the functionalists' view of the role of religion in society. Thus it probably would be more accurate simply to show that the study demonstrates the conflict and disruption resulting from different rates of change in two aspects of culture imposed upon the same social system.

REFERENCES CITED

Demerath, N. J., III, and R. A. Peterson, eds.

1967 System, Change, and Conflict: A Reader on . . . the Debate Over Functionalism. New York: Free Press.

Geertz, Clifford

1957 "Ritual and Social Change: A Javanese Example," American Anthropologist Vol. 59, No. 1, (Feb.), pp. 32-54.

1973 The Interpretation of Culture: Selected Essays. New York; Basic Books.

Keesing, Roger M.

1974 "Theories of Culture," in Siegel, B. J., A. R. Beals, and S. A. Tyler, eds. 1974.

Lessa, William A., and E. Z. Vogt, eds.

1958 Reader in Comparative Religion: An Anthropological Approach. New York: Harper and Row, 2nd ed., 1965; 3rd ed., 1973.

Malefijt, Annemarie de Waal

1974 Images of Man: A History of Anthropological Thought. New York: Knopf.

Malinowski, Bronislaw

1938 "Introductory Essay: The Anthropology of Changing African Culture," Methods of Study of Culture Contact in Africa. International Institute of African Languages and Cultures, Memorandu3 XV. Oxford University Press.

1945   The Dynamics of Culture Change: An Inquiry into Race Relations in Africa, Phyllis M. Kaberry, ed. New Haven: Yale University Press. (Much of Malinowski 1938 is incorporated in Part I.)

1948   Magic, Science and Religion and Other Essays. Garden City, New York: Doubleday Anchor Books.

Radcliffe-Brown, A. R.

1939   "Taboo," the Frazer Lecture of 1939, in Radcliffe-Brown, 1952.

1952   Structure and Function in Primitive Society: Essays and Addresses. Glencoe, Il.: Free Press.

Schneider, Louis, ed.

1964   Religion, Culture and Society: A Reader in the Sociology of Religion. New York: Wiley.

Siegel, B. J., A. R. Beals, and S. A. Tyler, eds.

1974   Annual Review of Anthropology. Palo Alto, Calif.: Annual Reviews, inc.

Yinger, J. Milton

1970   The Scientific Study of Religion. New York: Macmillan.

CHAPTER NINE

"Ethnicity as a Cultural System,"

Alice Higman Reich
Regis College

Abstract

Ethnicity has traditionally been studied as a consequence and concommitant of social stratification; ethnic culture has been regarded as a remnant, destined to disappear. The concept of ethnicity as a cultural system, conceptualizing a reasonable world, makes more sense in view of the recent rise of ethnic assertion. The paper explores the concept of ethnicity as a cultural system and applies it to Chicano ethnicity.

A woman who worked in a hotel spent her coffee breaks chatting with a friend. As it happened, they chatted in Spanish. A third woman was annoyed by this, because she could not understand Spanish, and she complained to their supervisor. The supervisor relayed the complaint to the Spanish-speaking women. "And now," said the woman telling the story, "we speak Spanish on purpose." This paper is about being ethnic on purpose, about the conscious use of ethnic identity and difference from others as a way of thinking about and being in the world.[1]

When I first began studying Spanish Americans, as they were called in Colorado in 1965, the literature addressed their ethnic culture as a problem, as a barrier to assimilation, and as a liability in contemporary American society. Assimilation was described as both inevitable and desirable for ethnic minorities in the United States; ethnic culture was seen as a conservative force which was destined to disappear. My own ethnographic experience over the succeeding twelve years coincided with a period of history during which Chicanos and other ethnic groups asserted their ethnic identity and redefined their ethnic culture as an asset, to be maintained and strengthened. Ethnicity, far from diminishing in importance, has become, in the words of Glazer and Moynihan, "a new social category as significant for the understanding of the present day world as that of social class itself."[2]

Ethnicity has taken on new meanings which require new modes of interpretation. In assessing the value of their ethnicity to various groups, anthropologists have begun to attend primarily to the psychological and social uses of ethnicity. The cultural dimension is noticeably absent from the majority of recent studies of ethnicity. It is the thesis of this paper that the analysis of ethnicity as a cultural system can make significant contributions to the understanding of ethnicity in general and to recent movements of ethnic assertion. After a brief review of the traditional, assimilationist view of ethnicity, and of the more current and more positive interpretations, I will discuss what it means to say that ethnicity is a cultural system and try to demonstrate the use of the model in understanding Chicano ethnicity.

Ethnicity — The Traditional View

Ethnicity refers to distinctness of culture, religion, nationality, and or language, and as such has some meaning with reference to all human groups everywhere. The real subject of the study of ethnicity is the relationship implied by the word "distinct." An ethnic group exists because of its difference from and its relationship to one or more other groups. Ethnic groups come into being through migrations, conquests, the formation of nations incorporating previously separate groups in their boundaries, and through the changing of national boundaries, all of which processes result in the interaction of different groups within the same ecological, economic, and or political sphere.

The relationships between ethnic groups are of two major kinds. Less frequently, ethnic groups are related in such a way that their ethnicity is not a basis for social stratification. Far more frequently, ethnic groups are related in such a way that they have structured unequal access to the things of value in a society. Because this is so often the case, "ethnic group" is sometimes used synonymously with "minority group" and means a group which differs in race, national origin, language, or culture from the group which is politically dominant in the society in which they both live.

Ethnic groups are distinguished within a larger society by appearance, by language, by dress, or by any of a variety of attributes. The attributes express and perpetuate the distinctiveness of the ethnic group.

Ethnic groups are relative in that they are defined in part by their relationship to other groups in the society, and they are subjective in that they are dependent upon the conceptions of the members themselves for their definition. Although biology is frequently the major metaphor of ethnicity, an ethnic group is primarily a social and cultural phenomenon, created and maintained by social and cultural processes.

An ethnic group is not a permanent, fixed entity. The composition of the group and its relationship to other groups can change over time. There are no easily definable, impermeable boundaries to ethnic groups; both individuals and whole groups can and do shift from one ethnic group identity to another.[3]

Sociologists have, until recently, been the major contributors to the study of minority groups and ethnic relations. Whatever their theoretical approach or major concern, most have regarded assimilation as both inevitable and desirable for minority groups in the United States. The classic statement is found in the Yankee City studies of Warner and Srole. In their analysis of immigrant groups in New England, they found that "each group enters the city at the bottom of the social heap and through several generations makes its desperate climb upward." The upward social mobility is accompanied by a loss of ethnic identity which, Warner and Srole conclude is the eventual outcome for all groups within the United States, though assimilation takes place at different rates for different groups.[4]

This prediction fit with the dominant theoretical orientation in sociology, with its emphasis on the transition from traditional society (based on ascribed characteristics and primordial ties such as kinship and ethnic group membership) to modern society (based on achieved statuses and rational associations such as social class and political interest groups).

Assimilation was seen not only as the theoretically inevitable end, but also a practical goal for ethnic minorities in the United States. Their ethnic culture was perceived as the major barrier between themselves and the achievement of success in the larger society. This view both grew out of and gave support to an ideology and cultural policy which emphasized conformity as the price of belonging in American society.[5]

The expectation that ethnic groups would gradually fade into insignificance has been called into question by the rise of what Schermerhorn calls "pluralistic competitive politics."[6] Ethnicity has shifted to the modern end of the continuum as it has beome a basis for the expression of political interest. And, very importantly, changes in the conceptions which ethnic group members hold of themselves have required changes in the perspectives from which scholars view ethnic groups. Banton suggests that the Black Power movement in the United States

> has upset the deterministic streak in the sociology of race relations, showing that the behavior of the subordinated is not completely determined by the social structure, for they have the power to choose the sort of group they will be.[7]

Ethnic groups have made it clear that they can no longer be regarded as simply a product of some set of social and historical conditions from which their futures can be predicted. They are part of a situation which is in part defined by their conceptions of themselves and of the situation. And human beings can change their conceptions; they in fact "have the power to choose the sort of group they will be." The fact that ethnic groups have chosen to be new sorts of groups has required a rethinking of concepts and methods in the study of ethnicity.

Ethnicity — New Perspectives

The study of ethnicity has increased tremendously since the middle of the 1960s. Books, journals, and ethnic studies programs all attest to a new interest in ethnic groups and in the ways in which they are studied. Anthropologists who are concerned with the relationships of ethnic groups to one another and to larger social systems frequently point to the publication of Barth's Ethnic Groups and Boundaries as a turning point in anthrpological theory. Barth's work pointed out the problematic aspects of ethnic boundaries and drew attention to the subjective nature of ethnic identity, giving rise to studies on the manipulation of symbols of ethnic identity. It also demonstrated the relationship of ethnicity to the larger systems of ecology, politics, and economics, giving rise to studies of the role ethnicity plays in regulating relationships between groups.[8] Since Barth, the anthropological perspective on ethnic groups has emphasized their role in social organization, in allocating and differentiating identities, statuses, and access to goods and services.

Ethnicity persists and is maintained because it has positive uses for members of ethnic groups and/or for the society in which they live. Anthropologists have studied ethnicity as a basis for maximizing the access of ethnic group members to environmental resources; as a basis for political organization; as a means of allocating economic roles; and as a source from which individuals derive necessary feelings of belonging to a group and of self worth.[9]

Most authors recognize that ethnicity has some cultural aspects, that it is taught, symbolized, or recognized culturally, but few look at the specifically cultural uses of ethnicity. Crumrine concerns himself with the symbolic nature of ethnic identity among the Mayo of Sonora, and points out that ethnic identity is based not on such things as language and dress, but on what those things mean in a larger interpretive system.[10] And Moerman, studying the Lue of Thailand, and Levy, studying a group of Lubovitcher Hassidim, describe the ways that individuals choose and use symbols of ethnic identity.[11] But when people look at the cultural dimension of ethnicity, the symbols of ethnic group membership, they rarely seem to be looking at a system which makes meaning out of the distinct kind of life experienced by members of ethnic groups.

Ethnicity as a Cultural System

It is very difficult to understand the meanings and uses of ethnicity, and particularly difficult to understand the recent assertion of their ethnicity on the part of so many groups in the United States, if ethnic culture is thought of as a remnant, a vestiage of a way of life which no longer exists, or even as a reflection of some more significant social, political, or economic relationship. It requires an appreciation of culture as a more significant force in human life. Such an appreciation of culture can be found in the works of Clifford Geertz.[12] Culture, as I understand Geertz' definition, is a system of beliefs, values, and ideas, encoded in symbols, learned and modified through social interaction. This system of meanings creates a conception of the world that is more real, more believable, and more believed in than that created by any other such system or than any objectively describable reality. The cultural system provides both a means of interpreting what is going on, a model of reality, and a guide to what should be going on, a model for reality.[13] Culture is shared, though obviously not equally by all members of any given group, and it has a compulsive quality, both in that, although an artifact of humans it seems "natural," and in that it has a moral force. Culture does not make people do things, but it guides and interprets behavior. And it is shaped and changed by behavior, but not determined by it.

Culture itself is a system, but it is also fruitful to think of its including a variety of cultural systems. The paradigmatic essay defining what a cultural system is and does is the essay "Religion as a Cultural System." In this essay Geertz argues that religion is one of a number of perspectives or ways of seeing and making sense of the world. The fundamental perspective is the perspective of common sense, "a simple acceptance of the world, its objects, and its processes as being just what they seem to be."[14] What they seem to be is, as Geertz points out, a cultural product. Each of us must have this common sense perspective to function in the world, a necessarily cultural world, in which we live. It is a ground of common understanding on which we move. But this common sense perspective leaves a number o problems unresolved and requires expansion through other perspectives. For example, the common sense perspective does not solve the problems of bafflement, evil, and suffering. And this gives rise, because of the need of humans to have their universe make sense, to the religious perspective. A religious perspective makes for its believers a real and believeable cosmic order in which all things are understandable, if not always understood. Other cultural systems expand on the common sense perspective in other ways, and, in turn, alter the common sense perspective.

The symbols of ethnic identity have always had meaning for members of ethnic groups which remained relatively uninvestigated in sociological and anthropological studies.[15] The symbols will vary from one population to another and can be discovered through enthnographic fieldwork. But the symbols themselves are far less important than the interpretive systems which they create. A study of the symbols of ethnicity should show that they are not either givens or simply justifications for action. Although they are useful as a basis for unification, as a strategy for political action, or as a way of maximizing access to resources, their primary purpose is to make up a conception of the world which provides a satisfying model of and model for the lives of the members of the ethnic group. Ethnicity, in other words, functions as a cultural system, making sense out of otherwise less than reasonable situations. The symbols of ethnic identity encode understandings which from the basis of identity: "Who am I?" and the basis for action: "What do I do?" and the basis for interpretation: "What is going on?"

The new ethnicity, defined by Bennett as "the proclivity of people to seize taditional cultural symbols as a definition of their own identity,"[16] (or by me as being ethnic on purpose) entails the reconceptualization of the meanings and uses of ethnic group membership. Movements of ethnic assertion have made ethnicity a consciously used perspective for interpreting and organizing experience. Ethnicity as a cultural system interprets the reality of ethnic group membership in a way which resolves a number of the paradoxes created by the common sense perspective of the dominant majority.

Where ethnic groups are low status groups, deprived of economic and political power, and deprived of social esteem, ethnic identity may come to be negatively valued, not only for the members of the dominant group or groups, but for the members of the ethnic groups themselves.[17] Symbols of ethnic group membership such as language or appearance take on a negative value, and the definition of what it means to be a member of a low status ethnic group comes to rest on negativity, either reactions to the dominant group, or absence of dominant group characteristics.

Where members of ethnic groups internalize much of the common sense perspective of the dominant group, it not only gives them a negative self image, it also poses a variety of other problems of meaning which require some resolution.[18]

Ethnic assertion creates a new interpretive system in which the symbols of ethnic identity take on a positive meaning for ethnic group members. This system conceptualizes a reasonable world, if not the best world, in which to live. And it interprets experience and guides action on the basis of ethnic group membership, but ethnic group membership as defined and valued by members themselves and not by the dominant majority. Ethnicity functions as a conceptual system which can, as Geertz says of ideology, "grasp, formulate, and communicate social realities which other cultural systems cannot."[19]

Chicano Ethnicity

Chicanos began the conscious construction of a culture based on their ethnic identity in the 1960s in order to resolve some of the major contradictions of their lives as members of a minority group in the United States. Their minority status, based on ethnic group membership, derives from historical and economic factors, processes through which Chicanos were clustered in low paying and low status occupations and isolated both physically and mentally from Anglo institutions and ideas.

Chicano ethnicity is based on a recognition of some shared Spanish-Mexican-Indian ancestry and the shared experience of being victims of discrimination in an Anglo dominated society. The symbols of Chicano ethnicity probably vary to some extent from one population to another though they generally include the Spanish language, Spanish surnames, a recognizable phenotype, some shared values about family life, and some shared tastes as for food and music. The reality of minority group membership, of being a part of a society in which there is a dominant group of which they are not members is the fundamental shared experience of Chicanos.

Chicanos are part of a society in which the majority group controls the wealth, holds the majority of powerful positions, profits most consistently from the existing educational and occupational structures, and defines what is culturally valued for the society as a whole.

One of the most powerful cultural tools the Anglo majority has had is its ideology of conformity to an Anglo model and assimilation as prerequisites to success in the society. This ideology was coupled with an unwillingness to allow such groups as Chicanos, blacks, and Native Americans to assimilate. The racism and discrimination used to block efforts of these groups are well chronicled. The double message, simultaneously demanding and blocking assimilation, has forced minority groups to compete in arenas in which whites make all the rules and minorities cannot win. The dominant majority is able to maintain its advantage while creating the illusion that success is available to all within the existing system. And this double message is the basis of the problems of meaning posed for members of minority groups by the common sense perspective of the dominant majority.

Chicanos have organized, protested, and acted against racism and discrimination since the nineteenth century, when the United States annexed the land on which Spanish and Mexicans had settled.[20] But these efforts took a new direction in the 1960s with the rise of the Chicano Movimiento. In the Movimiento, Chicano ethnicity was asserted and the symbols of ethnic identity were emphasized and reinterpreted positively to form a basis for self identification, group identification, and political action.

Many things happened in the 1960s which contributed to the Chicanos' movement of ethnic assertion, including the civil rights and Black Power movements, and, more directly, the War on Poverty. The government made ethnic identity the basis for legal and economic attention and gave ethnicity a positive value. One of the major tasks of the Movimiento in the face of this was the creation of Chicanos as a unified and visible ethnic group out of a number of previously distinct groups: Spanish Americans, Mexican Americans, Latin Americans, of different geographic and economic backgrounds. This required the construction and use of shared symbols of ethnic identity, the most obvious of which is the group name.

The emphasis on ethnic assertion, rather than solely political organization, or educational or economic achievement, is also related to other things going on both within the Chicano population and the larger society.

The supremacy of the Anglo ideal was under fire from Anglos as well as members of minority groups. There was dissatisfaction, confusion, and uncertainty about the way the society was working. Authority, national goals, and the means employed for attaining those goals were all called into question by the war in Viet Nam, by riots and protests of students and minority groups, and by countercultural movements. Peter Schrag has written about the failure of WASP values to provide emotional satisfaction, to extend humanity to significant numbers of human beings, or to achieve the promised material and technological successes for which emotion and humanity were sacrificed.[21]

After World War II, Chicanos tried "the American way" to a much greater extent than ever before. Their efforts to succeed were peaceful and accepting of the system, and they were not very successful.

There was considerable attention paid by social scientists of the 1960s to something they called "cultural deprivation" or "cultural deficiency." Persons attempting to understand some of the difficulties of minority groups in the educational and occupational systems engaged in "blaming the victim"[22] rather than looking to larger social structural causes of the problems of poverty and discrimination. Minority groups, through the culture they passed on to their children, were seen as the cause of their own problems. Minority group children were seen as culturally deprived because they had not been raised by Anglos, and that was thought to account for their failure in school and, later on, in life. Though the emphasis on cultural deprivation was, and is, wrongheaded, it helped create among minorities a self-conscious awareness about and a need for a new way of attending to their own cultural difference.

Specifically for Chicanos, this attention to cultural difference showed up some of the contradictions in the society in which they had been trying to operate. The social system was bearable, if not desirable, as long as it was perceived to work in the same way for everybody. Chicanos were willing to work a little bit harder and wait a little bit longer for their rewards. But as it became clear that the system did not work that way, the traditional conceptions of the relationship between minority groups and the dominant society became unacceptable, and new conceptions were required. All societies have lacks of fit, injustices, contradictions, and conflict. At the point at which these become intolerable, for whatever reasons, new systems of interpreting what it is that is going on are needed. The symbols of ethnic group membership are there, they have been there, symbolizing the social structural relationship, the economic differences, the political inequality. But these symbols are mobilized in a powerful new way which not only reinterprets the scene to make sense to large numbers of ethnic group members, but which is also at least potentially capable of restructuring the social relationships.

Through the Movimiento, Chicanos created an alternative order, one which would make more sense in terms of their life experiences, which would reveal and resolve some of the contradictions in the older order. These contradictions include the double binds of required conformity and assimilation coupled with racism and discrimination; of all the ways in which the system urges effort but rewards birth; of the value placed on learning foreign languages and the efforts to eradicate Spanish when it is a native language; of the beauty of brown skin, but only on white people.

The fundamental shared expereince of minority group members is that of being Other. Not all Chicanos speak Spanish, or have Spanish surnames, or "look Chicano," but all have known what it means to be a member of a minority group in an Anglo dominated society. The Chicano movement provides conscious models for ethnic group identification which are models of and models for behavior. These models heighten awareness of cultural differences between Chicanos and Anglos and imbue those differences with meaning and value. This means that Chicanos are no longer defined by Anglos, no longer "culturally deprived." Chicanos define themselves and cease to be simply a negative of Anglo culture.

The process of active self definition for Chicanos has involved their assertion of the rights to name themselves, to write their history and sociology, to decide what in their culture, their personalities, and their experience shall be valued positively and what negatively, and to construct and use the symbols of their ethnic identity. Without a positive emphasis on the symbols of ethnic difference, Chicanos are left with an ethnicity which is simply a consequence and concomitant of low social status and which can provide neither satisfaction for its members nor a basis for political organization.

The Chicano movement has meant that one can be a Chicano and that that has some meaning other than just "not Anglo." It has meant that one can think about the world in a way that makes the past valuable, the present understandable, and the future hopeful.

It is undoubtedly the case that the ethnicity of the Chicanos in the United States today is very important as a political strategy, as a means for maximizing power and thereby access to the valued goods of the society. It is also the case that movements of ethnic pride and assertion have important psychological functions in improving self esteem and creating positive group identity. But ultimately, I think, the Chicano movement came about because it was the only way to resolve a set of problems of meaning posed by ethnic minority group membership in a modern, ethnically stratified society.

The Chicano movement is directly concerned with the processes of cultural creation, in the construction of a positive Chicano identity, with the reinterpretation of the social structure by means of symbols of ethnic culture, and with group formation through the use of symbols in an attempt to unify previously diverse segments of the Spanish speaking population. This means that the study of ethnicity among Chicanos at this time is particularly illuminating of cultural processes. But these processes are not unique to Chicanos. All culture is a production of people in society; all cultural systems are used in organizing and interpreting experience. Ethnicity can be studied most fruitfully as an active process which does something for members of ethnic groups in modern society, not as a residue of traditional society. Culture itself needs to be examined as a process, and, as such, is not only a useful concept in understanding human life, but a necessary one.

FOOTNOTES

1. This paper is based on work done for my doctoral dissertation, The Cultural Production of Ethnicity: Chicanos in the University (Ph.D. dissertation. University of Colorado, 1977.) My intellectual debt to Clifford Geertz, whose student I was at The University of Chicago, is, I hope, obvious; my errors are my own.

2. Nathan Galzer and Daniel P. Moynihan, eds. Ethnicity: Theory and Experience (Cambridge: Harvard University Press, 1975), pp. 2-3.

3. Examples of this can be found in Frederik Barth, ed. Ethnic Groups and Boundaries (Boston: Little, Brown and Company, 1969) and E. R. Leach, Political Systems of Highland Burma (Boston: Beacon Press, 1965).

4. W. Lloyd Warner and Leo Srole, The Social Systems of American Ethnic Groups (New Haven: Yale University Press, 1945).

5. The pressure to conform exists alongside racism and systematic exclusion of certain groups from participation in much of the society. This point will be addressed below.

6. R. A. Schermerhorn, "Ethnicity in the Perspective of the Sociology of Knowledge," Ethnicity I (1):4.

7. Michael Banton, "1960: A Turning Point in the Study of Race Relations," Daedalus 103 (2):36.

8. Barth, Ethnic Groups and Boundaries.

9. There are a great number of recent works; on the use of ethnicity in maximizing access to environmental resources, see Leo A. Despres, ed. Ethnicity and Resource Competition in Plural Societies (The Hague: Mouton Publishers, 1975). Among the works on political uses of ethnicity are Michael Hechter, "The Political Economy of Ethnic Change," American Journal of Sociology 79 (5):1151-1178. and Lester Singer, "Ethnogenesis and Negro Americans Today," Social Research 29:419-432. An economic study is Brian Foster, "Ethnicity and Commerce," American Ethnologist I(3):437-448. And ethnicity as a source of self identification is found in George DeVos and Lola Romanucci-Ross, eds. Ethnic Identity: Cultural Continuity and Change. (Palo Alto: Mayfield Publishing Company, 1975).

10. N. Ross Crumrine, The House Cross of the Mayo Indians of Sonora, Mexico: A Symbol in Ethnic Identity, Anthropological Papers of the University of Arizona, No. 8.

11. Michael Moerman, "Accomplishing Ethnicity," in Ethnomethodology: Selected Readings ed. Roy Turner (Baltimore: Penguin Books, 1974). Sydelle Brooks Levy, "Shifting Patterns of Ethnic Identification among the Hassidim," in The New Ethnicity: Perspectives from Ethnology ed. John W. Bennett (St. Paul: West Publishing Company, 1975).

12. See particularly Clifford Geertz, The Interpretation of Cultures (New York: Basic Books, 1973).

13. Ibid., p. 93.

14. Ibid. p. 111.

15. I have discussed the meaning of their ethnicity for Spanish American villagers in "Spanish American Village Culture: Barrier to Assimilation or Integrative Force?" in Community Organization in Hispanic New Mexico ed. Paul Kutsche, Colorado College Studies.

16. Bennett, New Ethnicity, p. 1.

17. This is demonstrated in Judith Friedlander, Being Indiana in Hueyapan: A Study of Forced Identity in Contemporary Mexico, (New York: St. Martin's Press, 1975) and James O'Toole, Watts and Woodstock: Identity and Culture in the United States and South Africa. (New York: Holt, Rinehart and Winston, 1973).

18. These problems of meaning will be discussed in the section on Chicano ethnicity.

19. Geertz, Interpretation of Cultures, p. 210.

20. There are many good histories of Chicanos available. One very good one is Rodolfo Acuna, Occupied America: The Chicano Struggle Toward Liberation (San Francisco: Canfield Press, 1972).

21. Peter Schrag, The Decline of the Wasp (New York: Simon and Schuster, 1971).

22. William Ryan, Blaming the Victim (New York: Vintage Books, 1971).

BIBLIOGRAPHY

Acuna, Rodolfo. Occupied America: The Chicano Struggle Toward Liberation. San Francisco: Canfield Press, 1972.

Banton, Michael. "1960: A Turning Point in the Study of Race Relations." Daedalus 103 (2):31-44.

Barth, Frederik, ed. Ethnic Groups and Boundaries. Boston: Little, Brown and Company, 1969.

Bennett, John W., ed. The New Ethnicity: Perspectives from Ethnology. St. Paul, Minnesota: West Publishing Company, 1975.

Crumrine, N. Ross. The House Cross of the Mayo Indians of Sonora, Mexico: A Symbol in Ethnic Identity. Anthropological Papers of the University of Arizona, No. 8.

Despres, Leo A., ed Ethnicity and Resource Competition in Plural Societies. The Hague: Mouton Publishers, 1975.

DeVos, George and Romanucci-Ross, Lola, eds., Ethnic Identity: Cultural Continuity and Change. Palo Alto: Mayfield Publishing Company, 1975.

Foster, Brian L. "Ethnicity and Commerce." American Ethnologist I(3):437-448.

Friedlander, Judith. Being Indian in Hueyapan: A Study of Forced Identity in Contemporary Mexico. New York: St. Martin's Press, 1975.

Geertz, Clifford. The Interpretation of Cultures. New York: Basic Books, 1973.

Glazer, Nathan and Moynihan, Daniel P., eds. Ethnicity: Theory and Experience. Cambridge: Harvard University Press, 1975.

Hechter, Michael. "The Political Economy of Ethnic Change." American Journal of Sociology 79 (5):1151-1178.

Kutsche, Paul, ed. Community Organization in Hispanic New Mexico. Colorado Springs: Colorado College Studies (forthcoming).

Leach, E. R. Political Systems of Highland Burma. Boston: Beacon Press, 1965.

Levy, Sydelle Brooks. "Shifting Patterns of Ethnic Identification among the Hassidim." In The New Ethnicity: Perspectives from Ethnology, John W. Bennett, ed. St. Paul, Minnesota: West Publishing Company, 1975.

Moerman, Michael. "Accomplishing Ethnicity." In Ethnomethodology: Selected Readings, Roy Turner, ed. Baltimore: Penguin Books, 1974.

O'Toole, James. Watts and Woodstock: Identity and Culture in the United States and South Africa. New York, Holt, Rinehard and Winston, 1973.

Reich, Alice Higman. The Cultural Production of Ethnicity: Chicanos in the University. (Ph. D. Dissertation, University of Colorado, 1977).

"Spanish American Village Culture: Barrier to Assimilation of Integrative Force?" In Community Organization in Hispanic New Mexico, Paul Kutsche, ed. Colorado Springs: Colorado College Studies (forthcoming).

Ryan, William. Blaming the Victim. New York: Vintage Books, 1971.

Schermerhorn, R. A. "Ethnicity in the Perspective of the Sociology of Knowledge." Ethnicity I (1):1-14.

Schrag, Peter. The Delcine of the Wasp. New York: Simon and Schuster, 1971.

Warner, W. Lloyd and Srole, Leo, eds. The Social Systems of American Ethnic Groups. New Haven: Yale University Press, 1945.

CHAPTER TEN

"Meaning as Hermeneutics: The Interpretational Imperative,"

John H. Morgan
University of Texas

MEANING AS HERMENEUTICS:

The Interpretational Imperative*

Everywhere in the modern world is evidenced an almost frantic compulsion for man-kind to understand himself and his world. Whether we peruse the latest works in laterature, art, or music, the result is the same — man seeks to understand himself and his world. But such understanding, though sought after with passionate drive, continually eludes him. "The tragedy of modern man," says Abraham J. Heschel in venturing to explain modern man's present crisis, "is that he thinks alone."[1] In mankind's frantic search to understand himself and his relationship to his world, he is continually baffled and mystified by his persisting inability to define himself in terms relevant to his humanity, terms larger than himself with power to draw him forward into the future. "The greatest challenge of modern man," explains Teilhard de Chardin, "is to establish an abiding faith in the future."[2]

But in order for such a faith to emerge, man must not only have a singularly per-sonal sense of "What am I?" but also a universally social sense of "Who is Man?" "No age," observes Martin Heidegger, "has known so much, and so many different things, about man as ours . . . And no age has known less than ours of what man is."[3] The problem, as Heidegger so clearly sees, is not a deficiency in technical

---

*To the graduate faculties of Yale University, where I began this study, as a Post-doctoral Research Fellow, the University of Chicago where I continued my work as a Postdoctoral Scholar in Residence, and Princeton, where I completed this paper, as a Visiting Fellow, I am deeply appreciative. I wish especially to thank Professor Clifford Geertz of the Institute for Advanced Studies at Princeton for his positive evaluation of my treatment of his thought.

knowledge, in scientific information, in bio-medical and psycho-social aptitude and insight, but rather the problem is deeper and lies behind all this burgeoning of knowledge, information, aptitudes and insights. The problem is not man's intellect. The problem is man himself. Knoweldge of the world seems not to be a problem, but the understanding of man himself and his realtionship to the world does. "We are the first epoch," observes Scheler, "in which man has become fully and thoroughly 'problematic' to himself; in which he no longer knows what he essentially is, but at the same time also knows that he does not know."[4]

Of course, to know that one does not know is one step towards addressing the problem responsibly. What seems to be absent from the modern experience is any context or frame of reference within which or from which judgements can be made with conviction, a position from which lives can be lived with authenticity. "The most poignant problem of modern life," explains the Nobel Prize wining biologist, Rene Dubos, "is probably man's feeling that life has lost significance."[5] The gradual encroachment of pervasive relativism — a sense that nothing is any more or less significant than anything else — seems to have successfully assaulted man's own self-image moreso than any of his particular ideologies or industries.

And when man looks to his ancient past for some root from which to regain strength to carry on and renew his vigor to reaffirm the humanness of his being, mankind falters. What was perceived in days of resoluteness to be way-markers in man's self-understanding degenerates in days of self-doubt to little more than half-hearted speculations. When men are strong, they revere their past for the power they see there; but when men falter, their past too loses power. As the French Philosopher Ernst Cassirer has so painfully pointed out, "Nowhere in Plato's Socratic dialogues do we find a direct solution to the problem, 'What is man?' There is only an indirect answer, 'Man is declared to be that creature who is constantly in search of himself — a creature who in every moment of his existence must examine and scrutinize the conditions of his existence."[6]

From Plato we learn little about the nature of man, but we learn much about that which makes man human. His humanity is manifest in his drive to know, as Aristotle once said centuries ago — to know who he is and what his relationship is to the world. "He is a being in search of meaning," says Heschel.[7] And, in seeking to know himself, man defines his world. He interprets his world in terms of his own humanity. Throughout history, the human crisis has always centered around man's search for himself, for meaning, a meaning which derives from his propensity to interpret. By virtue of interpreting his world, man creates a history and history for man is the record of his discovery of meaning for himself within his world. And meaning in turn becomes the mechanism whereby he continues to understand and interpret. A discussion of this development, of man interpreting himself and his world in terms of relationship-as-meaning, is the purpose of this paper.

In man's quest to understand himself, in his drive to examine and scrutinize the conditions of his existence, to come to grips with his world, he must inevitably engage in interpretation. Man confronts a world of reality which, if he is to survive and thrive, he must interpret. The issue is not so much whether he creates or discovers order and purpose in thie world of reality as the fact that this reality (real or imagined) compels him to encounter it and interpret it. "I believe," says Marias, "that the universe is covered by a patina of interpretations."[8] Of course, what is not being implied here is that reality is merely interpretation. On the contrary, "reality is something that makes me make interpretation (emphasis mine)." The human quality of the lived experience in the world of reality is fundamentally interpretational. Man never achieves a sense of this reality without interpretation.

Amidst this frantic compulsion to know himself by means of interpreting the world, we must not suppose that mankind's humanity has any analogue in the physical environment from which to draw comparisons. Whereas the physical — the sub-human environment — can be described in terms of its objective properties, Cassirer argues cogently that "man may be described and defined only in terms of his counsciousness."[9] That which so decisively differentiates the physical world of reality from the human world of reality is consciousness — man's reflective self-awareness. Teilhard de Chardin once observed that the difference between man and animal is that the latter "knows" but the former "knows that he knows."[10]

Though man, as animal, encounters his world as a physical reality, man, as human, encounters his world as an interpreted reality. This distinctiveness of man vis a vis animal is not merely a quantitative leap in breadth of worlds perceived but is a qualitative leap in depth of worlds experienced. Whereas man like other animals employs receptor and effector systems of bio-physical adaptation to his physical environment, man alone has discovered the symbolic system as explained so cogently by by Cassirer. "This new acquisition transforms the whole of human life . . . As compared with other animals man lives not merely in a broad reality; he lives, so to speak, in a new dimension of reality."[11] We might wish to call this a milieu symbolicum.

This new dimension of reality is a discovery of man resulting from his drive to interpret his world — an encounter with the symbolic dimension of a world perceived in abstract space. This is the distinctive character of the human species, that it has developed the capacity for abstraction through symbolization, and in abstracting from the physical world man interprets the symbolic world known only to himself. And herein lies the humanness of man's encounter with and desire to understand this new dimension, this symbolic world, which demands not only a subject-object encounter but an interpretation. "Wherever a man dreams or raves," explains Paul Ricouer, "another man arises to give an interpretation; what was already discourse, even if incoherent, is brought into coherent discourse by hermeneutics."[12] Man manifests his humanity by interpreting, not just reacting, to his environment, i.e., human experience seeking understanding.

As noted earlier, the modern crisis is one of meaning, man's inability to interpret his world in a manner that makes what he does, thinks, and dreams make a difference. "The concept of meaning," suggests Langer, "in all its varieties, is the dominant philosophical concept of our time."[13] The dominance of the concept of meaning bespeaks the pervasiveness of the perceived problem. Man is in search of his own humanity, or in the words of Carl Gustav Jung, "Modern man in search of a soul."[14]

And in the search, and within the new dimension of symbol, mankind requires a sense of orderliness, predictability, rationality, understandability. "Men are congenitally compelled," says Berger, "to impose a meaningful order upon reality."[15] Though I had rather say man is compelled to discover a meaningful order within reality, nevertheless, the "propensity for order . . . (is) one fundamental human trait" which is crucial in understanding the compulsions of man to interpret as meaningful the world of reality.[16]

It should be evident by now that what I mean by understanding through interpretation is not simply an explanation of the world as man encounters it. Long ago, Dilthey cleared up the matter of distinguishing between explanation and understanding as applied to the human species. "We explain," says he, "by means of purely intellectual processes, but we understand by means of the combined activities of all the mental powers in apprehending . . . We explain nature; man we must understand (emphasis mine)."[17] We can say then that in the act of understanding man's nature, he comes through mental effort to comprehend living human experience.

Only man can have a crisis of meaning for only man can understand his world by interpreting the complexities of his encounter with the new dimension of the milieu symbolicum. And in this dimension, which he interprets, man confronts the historical nature of his being in the world. Richard Palmer has aided us along this train of thought by focusing not only upon Cassirer's description of man's animal symbolicum but also and concomitantly upon man's compulsion to interpret this new dimension of reality. "In hermeneutical theory," Palmer explains, "man is seen as dependent on constant interpretation of the past, and thus it could almost be said that man is the 'hermeneutical animal," who understands himself in terms of interpreting a heritage and shared world bequeathed him from the past, a heritage constantly present and active in all his actions and decisions.[18] It is in historical consciousness that man becomes fully human and necessarily confronts his own humanness. By virtue of his compulsion to interpret a world he desires to understand, a world limited to his capacity for abstraction through symbolization, man discovers history. "In historicality," says Palmer, "modern hermeneutics finds its theoretical foundations."

In man's desire to know, to come not merely to an explanation of his physical environment but to understand by interpretation the symbolic dimension of reality which he alone has discovered, he is inevitably confronted with the emergence of an historical consciousness. "Man has no nature," Ortega y Cassett once said, "what he has is history."[19] Certainly what has been presented here thus far is not so much an attempt to definitionally circumscribe human nature so much as to characterize the human propensity as interpretational, as hermeneutical, as symbolic, as historical. Heidegger said in deference to Dilthey's enamoration of history that "historical understanding is something belonging to the way of being man." We have seen that with the emergence of consciousness, i.e., reflective self-awareness, within the human species a new dimension of reality has been discovered, understood, and interpreted such that an historical sensibility is an inevitable and indispensable correlary of man's own humanity.

With the overall effort here being to illustrate that man's propensity to interpret his world rests upon a sense of history as meaning and meaning as hermeneutic, Palmer has said that the "hermeneutical experience is intrinsically historical."[20] As noted earlier, man, unlike animal, confronts an objective world which he encounters not only with his receptor and effector sensory systems, but unlike other animals, man also and distinguishingly encounters an abstract world of symbols. "Ideal reconstruction," says Cassirer, "not empirical observation, is the first step in historical knowledge . . . (For) the historian finds at the very beginning of his research a symbolic universe."[21] It is at the level of historical knowledge that man so uniquely distinguishes himself above the physical world of animal life. Man interprets what he encounters, and his interpretation is historical in character.

The interpretation of man's place in the world is essentially an expression of his perception of relationships — relationships as embodying a sense of life's meaning. "The component parts of what comprises our view of the progression of our life (Auschauung des Lebensverlaufes)," explains Dilthey, "are all contained together in living itself."[22] Whereas Kantians would have us believe that this inner temporality or historicality is superimposed from a priori mental categories, we would rather argue for their being intrinsic to man's world as Dilthey and Heidegger, among others, have so convincingly argued in modern times. The point is crucial to all hermeneutics and is determinative for this paper. "Experience," explains Palmer, "is intrinsically temporal (historical), and therefore understanding of experience must also be in commensurately temporal categories of thought."[23]

Historicality (Geschichtlichkeit) as used here is formed by Dilthey's thesis that "what man is only history can tell him."[24] The term usually carries a dual meaning, discussed at length by Otto Friedrich Bollnow, viz., first, the fact that man understands himself not so much through introspection as through the objectification of life, and second, that man's nature is not a fixed essence but rather that in the phrase of Dilthey, man is a "not-yet-determined animal" (noch nicht festgestellte tier).[25] Thus we see the inevitability of man's interpretation of his world, being an expression of his quest for meaning, as an historical event. The intrinsic temporality of understanding itself, as Heidegger has argued, is in seeing the world always in terms of past, present, and future. This we are calling the historicality of understanding. "Meaning," Palmer has suggested, "always stands in a horizontal context . . . (such that) the concept of 'historicality' . . . comes to refer not only to man's dependence on history for his self-understanding and self-interpretation but also to the inseparability of history and the intrinsic temporality of all understanding."[26] `

Understanding, Heidegger has taught us, is the basis for all interpretation. By understanding, he would have us mean man's power to grasp his own "possibilities for being" within the "lifeworld of our existence." As Heidegger sees it, understanding operates within a set of already interpreted releationships, or in Heidegger's own term, "relational whole (Bewandtnisganzheit)." And, whereas understanding implies interpreted relationships, Dilthey has earlier suggested that meaningfulness is always a matter of reference to a "context of relationships (Strukturzusammenhaug)."

Historicality as man's interpretation of his perceived relationships to the world and himself manifests itself in terms of man's quest for meaning. Human history, we are suggesting, is the result of man's interpretation of perceived relationships — his grasp through interpretation of meaning. "History," Cassirer once said, "is relationship (meaning) understood." Meaning is the essence of history as history is the essence of human interpretation of the new dimension of reality, a dimension which can only be understood and interpreted in terms of the experiential category of meaning. "Meaning," continues Palmer, "is the name given to different kinds of relationships."[27]

It is at this juncture, of history as meaning, that man's nature so poignantly manifests and reveals itself. In grasping his world — relation as meaning — man grasps himself, the maker of history and the discoverer of its meaning. "History is not knowledge of external facts or events," explains Cassirer, "it is a form of self-knowledge . . . In history man constantly returns to himself."[28] As man is compelled to interpret his newly discovered milieu symbolicum, he comes to know that the meaning of history is most exactly the history of meaning, a process whereby man interpreting his abstract environment comes to a working definition of himself. "Not through introspection," says Dilthey, "but only through history do we come to know ourselves."[29]

It is through interpretation, says Heidegger, that man confronts the problem and meaning of his own being. "The logos of a phenomenology of Dasein," explains Heidegger, "has the character of hermeneuein (to interpret), through which are made known to Dasein the structure of his own being and the authentic meaning of being given in his (preconscious) understanding of being."[30] Therefore, we might convincingly argue that historicality — man's consciousness of the sequential nature of interpretation — constitutes the proper milieu for man's self-understanding. And, therefore, in interpretation, i.e., hermeneutics, we find man's best efforts at finding, within the context of the quest for meaning the nature of his own being. "Phenomenology of Dasein," continues Heidegger, "is hermeneutics in the original sense of the words, which designates the business of interpretation . . . Hermeneutics," concludes Heidegger, "has become interpretation of the being of Dasein."

If Heidegger has strengthened our belief that hermeneutics as interpretation of the being of Dasein is indispensable in man's quest for self-knowledge, then Dilthey has vindicated our sense of history as meaning, the experiential framework of relationships embodying the meaningfulness of existence interpreted and understood. In experience itself, temporality is expressed in the context of relationship, for experience is not a static phenomenon, but rather, "in its unity of meaning it (experience) tends to reach out and encompass both recollection of the past and anticipation of the future in the total context of 'meaning'."[31]

Historical consciousness emerged within the context of a human enperience of compulsion to interpret the abstracted relationships and realities of a symbolic world. And in the emergence of this consciousness, man came to realize that the meaning of this compulsion, the meaning of this history was really the history of man's meaning. "Meaning," Dilthey pointed out, "cannot be imagined . . . (rather) the past and the future form a structural unity with the presentness of all experience, and perception in the present is interpreted."[32] In this discovery of meaning, revealed in history to man through his drive to know his world by interpreting it, man has discovered the means by which life can be grasped. The meaning of the being of Dasein is within human reach.

The crisis of modern man we have been saying is a crisis of meaning. Man, due to techno-scientific and psycho-cosmic factors which will not be analyzed here, has lost of capacity not to explain but to understand his world and to interpret his relationship to it meaningfully. A failure of historical consciousness has bludgeoned man into a state of existential unconsciousness. The task for modern man, if he would regain a sense of resolute purposefulness and unequivocal directionability to his life, is to recover a consciousness of historicality (Geschichtlichkeit) of his own existence. Dilthey has convincingly suggested that life is experience in "individual moments of meaning," and that these moments of meaning "require the context of the past and the horizon of future expectations . . . " which can only be explained and understood in terms of the human dimension of historicality.[33] An understanding of the character and quality, origin and direction, of these "moments of meaning" is what our discussion of man as interpreter, interpretation as history, and history as meaning is all about. To illustrate how the concept of meaning can be employed as a hermeneutical device in grasping the meaning of our being is our last and pivotal point in this discussion, viz. meaning as hermeneutics.

The humanness of man is exemplified in his drive and ability to encounter and interpret a new dimension of reality beyond the physical environment, a world of symbols embodying an intrinsically historical discovery of meaning. Not only does human life illustrate the meaning of history, human life also embodies the history of meaning. "The dimension of meaning," explains Heschel, "is as indigenous to man's being human as the dimension of space is to stars and stones."[34] If our scenario is correct this far — man as interpreter, interpretation as history, history as meaning — then we are led resolutely to the crowning postulate of this development which is that meaning for man, whether created or discovered, is the interpretive mechanism par excellence by which he lives. Meaning is hermeneutics.

Technically speaking, "hermeneutics is the study of understanding," or more precisely, hermeneutics "is the study of the methodological principles of interpretation and explanation." Yet, though these definitions are correct in the academic sense of the word, they fail to reach at the heart of my intention. They fall short of the existentially human quality of my aphorism — meaning as hermeneutics. Closer to the point is Ricouer's suggestion that "hermeneutics is the system by which the deeper significance is revealed beneath the manifest content."[36]

Our intention in developing this thought has led us to Heidegger's notion of the "hermeneutics of Dasein" outlined in his <u>Sein und Zeit</u> (1927). Here, we see the temporality and existential roots of understanding which form the backdrop for man's interpretation of the maningfulness of his being. Hermeneutics for Heidegger is the study of the understanding of the works of man, or more pointedly, an explanation of human existence itself. Interpretation as well as understanding are foundational modes of man's being. And the followers of Heidegger see hermeneutics as a philosophical exploration of the character and requisite conditions for all understanding and interpretation.[37]

Heidegger's contribution to hermeneutics is unquestionably significant, having marked a turning point in the development of both the term and the field. Hermeneutics
has become at once linked both to the ontological and the existential dimensions
of understanding and interpretation. Now, the definition of hermeneutics, thanks to
Heidegger, deals with "the moment that meaning comes to light." In these moments,
man interprets his world in terms of meaning, i.e., meaning as hermeneutics. And,
these moments, as expressive of the historicality of man, are both cultural and religious in the sense that culture and religion are meaning-systems by means of which
man grasps the new dimension of his own being in the world.

Meaning, as discussed earlier, carries with it the element of historicality, of temporality. Meaning does not exist merely in the abstract but profoundly manifests
itself in the concrete, in the lived experience of the human community. Necessarily,
then, if meaning is to function hermeneutically as the human mechanism for interpreting the world, meaning must function through those arenas of human experience
most directly linked to encountering a world in need of interpretation. Those arenas
are culture and religion.

The Princeton anthropologist, Clifford Geertz, has defined "man as a symbolizing,
conceptualizing, meaning-seeking animal,"[38] who produces culture and religion as
expressions of these characteristics. Culture, explains Geertz, is "an historically
transmitted pattern of meanings embodied in symbols."[39] Accordingly, religion "is
in part an attempt to conserve the fund of general meanings in terms of which each

individual interprets his experience and organizes his conduct." In the same context, Geertz has suggested that man's compulsion to "make sense out of experience" is as characteristically human as man's biological needs. Thus, "to make sense out of experience" is what in the Heideggerian sense we are labelling hermeneutics, and it is by means of the meaning-systems of culture and religion that this "drive to interpret" most predictably, systematically, and fruitfully reveals itself.

We have been suggesting that meaning is the hermeneutical device or key by which man interprets his world in the sense that hermeneutics in the Heideggerian usage is "the analysis of human existence."[40] Whereas among the anthropologists, Geertz would propose that culture-analysis must focus upon the meaning-system embodied in cultural symbols, philosophers and theologians might likewise argue that religious-analysis must focus upon the meaning-system embodied in religious symbols. Heinrich Otto, a modern theologian, reportedly has said that "theology is really hermeneutics," whereas Carl Michaelson, another modern theologian, has suggested that systematic theology is "the hermeneutical analysis of being."

If Geertz is the modern anthropological exemplar of culture-analysis employing the concept of meaning as the interpretive key in his science, then Paul Tillich is unquestionably the modern theological exemplar of religious analysis employing the concept of meaning as the interpretive key in his discipline.[41] For Tillich, meaning is that from which all religious and cultural expressions receive their impetus. And he was, therefore, very impatient with any notion of a meaningless existence — for him a notion impossible to entertain or defend. "Even the totality of meaning," Tillich once argued, "need not be meaningful, but rather could disappear, like every particular meaning in the abyss of meaninglessness, if the presupposition of an unconditional meaningfulness were not alive in every act of meaning."[42] For Tillich, to raise the question or possibility of meaninglessness is to have already posited meaning.

Contrary to Sartre's existentialism,[43] Tillich insists that meaning is not a creation of man's own devices but rather a discovery which reveals the sustaining source of the human spirit. "Culture," reasons Tillich, "does not create this empty space of mere validity. It creates meaning as the actualization of what is potential in the bearer of the spirit — in man."[44] Culture is not self-contained but rather points beyond its symbol-systems to that from which it derives its power for human creativity. Tillich argues that both culture and religion are meaning-systems, are mechanisms expressed through symbols by the human spirit, which converge in the creativity of man's quest to interpret his world. "Religion," he explains, "is directedness toward the Unconditional (the Unconditional meaning, toward the import of meaning), and culture is directedness toward the conditioned forms (of meaning) and their unity."[45] Having framed the relationship of culture and religion in terms of their shared convergence upon meaning as man's effort to grasp his world, Tillich has added another dimension to Geertz's approach to culture and religion analysis. Thus, Tillich establishes a symbiotic relationship between religion and culture in these terms: "In the cultural act, the religious is substantial; in the religious act, the cultural is formal."[46]

If culture is the experiential expression of meaning, or more correctly is the context within which and the socio-historical mechanism whereby meaning is both experienced and expressed, then the function of the concept of meaning is necessarily interpretational, or hermeneutical.[47] In closing, we might suggest that religion as an expression of meaning is a demonstration of mankind's quest to know and understand his world and his place in it. We might then, on the basis of the foregoing discussion, propose a set of definitions. Culture is that integrated complex of conceptual and empirical expressions of conditional and created meaning embodied within a socio-historical milieu. Religion is that integrated complex of conceptual and empirical expressions of unconditional and discovered meaning embodied within a socio-historical milieu.[48] By having defined religion and culture as meaning-systems, as arenas within which expressions of meaning converge, we have demonstrated the religio-cultural matrix of interpretation — an interpretation of man's historicality wherein we can define religion and culture as meaning, and meaning as hermeneutics.

FOOTNOTES

1. Abraham Joshua Heschel, Who Is Man? (Stanford, CA: Stanford University Press, 1968), p. 76.

2. Teilhard de Chardin, Building the Earth (N.Y.: Avon Books, 1965). p. 105.

3. Martin Heidegger, Kant und das Problem der Metaphysik (Frankfort: Klostermann, 1951).

4. As quoted in Martin Buber, Between Man and Man (N.Y.: Macmillan, 1968), p. 182.

5. Rene Dubos, So Human An Animal (N.Y.: Charles Scribner's Sons, 1968), p. 14.

6. Ernst Cassirer, An Essay on Man (New Haven: Yale University Press, 1969), p. 5.

7. Abraham Joshua Heschel, The Insecurity of Freedom: Essays on Human Existence (N. Y.: Schocken Books, 1972), p. 162.

8. Julian Marias, "Philosophic Truth and the Metaphoric System," in Interpretation: The Poetry of Meaning, edited by Stanley Romaine Hopper and D. L. Miller (N.Y.: Harcourt, Brace & World, 1967), p. 48.

9. Cassirer, Essay on Man, p. 5.

10. For discussion, see my "Ethnicity and the Future of Man: The Perspective of Teilhard de Chardin," The Teilhard Review, XI, 1 (Feb., 1976): 16-21.

11. Cassirer, Essay on Man, p. 24.

12. Paul Ricouer, "The Symbol Gives Rise to Thought," in Literature and Religion, edited by. G. B. Gunn (N.Y.: Harper Forum, 1971), p. 213.

13. Susanne K. Langer, Philosophical Sketches (N.Y.: Mentor Books, 1964), p. 54.

14. Carl Gustav Jung, Modern Man in Search of a Soul (N.Y.: Harcourt, Brace, and World, 1933).

15. Peter L. Berger, the Sacred Canopy: Elements of a Sociological Theory of Religion (N. Y.: Anchor, 1969), p. 22.

16. Peter L. Berger, A Rumor of Angels: Modern Society and the Rediscovery of the Sacred (N.Y.: Anchor, 1970), p. 53.

17. Wilhelm Dilthey, Gesammelte Schriften, 14 volumes (Gottingen: Vandenhoeck and Ruprecht, 1913-1967), V: 172.

18. Richard E. Palmer, Hermeneutics: Interpretation Theory in Schleiermacher, Dilthey, Heidegger, and Gadamer (Evanston, IL: Northwestern University Press, 1969), p. 118. Also see my "Religious Myth and Symbol: A Convergence of Philosophy and Anthropology," Philosophy Today, XVIII, 4 (Spring, 1974): 68-84.

19. As quoted in Cassirer, Essay on Man, p. 172.

20. Palmer, Hermeneutics, p. 242.

21. Cassirer, Essay on Man, pp. 174-175.

22. Dilthey, Gesammelte Schriften, VII: 140.

23. Palmer, Hermeneutics, p. 111.

24. Dilthey, Gesammelte Schriften, VIII; 224.

25. Otto Friedrich Bollnow, Die Lebensphilosophie (Berlin: Springer, 1958).

26. Palmer, Hermeneutics, p. 117.

27. Ibid., p. 120.

28. Cassirer, Essay on Man, p. 191.

29. Dilthey, Gesammelte Schriften, VII: 279.

30. Martin Heidegger, Sein Und Ziet (Halle: Niemeyer, 1927), p. 37.

31. Dilthey as quoted by Palmer, Hermeneutics, p. 109.

32. Dilthey, Gesammelte Schriften, VI: 317.

33. Dilthey as quoted by Palmer, Hermeneutics, p. 101.

34. Heschel, Who Is Man?, p. 51.

35. Webster's Third New International Dictionary.

36. Palmer, Hermeneutics, p. 44.

37. Heidegger's hermeneutics is carefully analyzed by Hans-Gerog Gadamer, Wahrheit und Methode: Grundzuge einer Philosophischen Hermeneutik (Tubingen: J. C. B. Mohr, 1960).

38. Clifford Geertz, "Ethos, World-View and the Analysis of the Sacred Symbols," Antioch Review (Winter, 1957-58): 436.

39. Clifford Geertz, "Religion as a Cultural System," in Anthropological Approaches to the Study of Religion, edited by M. Banton (Longon: Tavistock, 1966), p. 3.

40. Stanley Romaine Hopper, "The Poetry of Meaning," in Literature and Religion, p. 223.

41. For a critical comparison of Tillich and Geertz on this point, see my "Re-

42. Paul Tillich, What Is Religion? (N.Y.: Harper, 1969), p. 57.

43. For a critique of Sartre's use of the concept of "meaning," see my In Search of Meaning: From Freud to Teilhard de Chardin (Washington; D. C.: University Press of America, 1978), pp. 15-23.

44. Paul Tillich, Systematic Theology, 3 volumes (Chicago: University of Chicago Press, 1967), III: 84.

45. Tillich, What Is Religion?. p. 59.

46. Ibid., p. 60.

47. See my "Clifford Geertz: An Interfacing of Anthropology and Religious Studies," Horizons, V, 2 (Winter, 1978): 203-210.

48. This point is considered carefully in my "Theology and Symbol: An Anthropological Approach," Journal of Religious Thought, XXX, 3 (Fall, 1974): 51-61.

EDITOR AND CONTRIBUTORS

John H. Morgan, (Ph.D., Hartford), formerly Scholar-in-Residence at The University of Chicago and Postdoctoral Research Fellow at Yale University, is currently Associate Professor and Chairman of the Department of Behavioral Science at Jarvis Christian College and Adjunct Graduate Professor at The University of Texas at Tyler where this collection of essays was brought to publication under a grant from the National Science Foundation. This project was conceived during a postdoctoral appointment as Visiting Fellow at Princeton where Dr. Morgan undertook a thorough study of Geertz's works. Elected a Fellow of the American Anthropological Association in 1974, Dr. Morgan has taught graduate anthropology at The University of Connecticut and philosophy at The University of Hartford. He has published in such periodicals as Encounter, The Journal of Religion, Philosophy Today, The Teilhard Review, Social Science, International Review of History and Political Science, International Review of Cross-Cultural Studies, the American Benedictine Review, Journal of Religion and Health, Horizons, and Worldview. His latest book is entitled, In Search of Meaning: From Freud to Teilhard de Chardin.

John P. Thorp, Ph.D.
Assistant Professor of Anthropology
St. Mary's College
Notre Dame, IN 46556

James Preston, Ph.D.
Assistant Professor of Anthropology
SUNY-College
Oneonta, NY 13820

E. Jean Langdon, Ph.D.
Department of Anthropology
Cedar Crest College
Allentown, PA 18104

Ann Marie Powers, Ph.D. Cand.
Lecturer in Anthropology
State University of New York
Stony Brook, NY

Fritz Holscher, M.A.
Department of Sociology
University of South Africa
Pretoria, South Africa

James O. Buswell, III, Ph.D.
Professor of Anthropology
Wheaton College
Wheaton, IL 60187

Alice Higman Reich, Ph.D.
Assoc. Prof. of Anthropology
Regis College
Denver, CO. 80221

John H. Morgan, Ph.D.
506 Viewcrest
Longview, TX 75604